AMAZING
SOLAR SYSTEM
PROJECTS
YOU CAN BUILD YOURSELF

Delano Lopez

Nomad Press
A division of Nomad Communications
10 9 8 7 6 5 4 3 2 1
Copyright © 2008 by Nomad Press

ISBN: 9781934670002

Nebulae image on page 94 courtesy of NASA/JPL-Caltech
All illustrations by Shawn Braley

Questions regarding the ordering of this book should be addressed to
Independent Publishers Group
814 N. Franklin St.
Chicago, IL 60610
www.ipgbook.com

Nomad Press
2456 Christian St.
White River Junction, VT 05001

Contents

Timeline

About 13.7 Billion Years Ago The universe is created from the Big Bang.

About 4.6 Billion Years Ago The solar system forms.

150 BCE Ptolemy writes the *Almagest* describing the geocentric (earth-centered) model of the solar system.

1542 CE Copernicus writes *On the Revolutions of the Heavenly Spheres,* which describes the solar system as heliocentric, or sun centered.

1609 Johannes Kepler publishes *New Astronomy* based in part on the observations of Tycho Brahe. In this book, Kepler argues that the planets travel around the sun in elliptical orbits.

1610

Galileo Galilei is the first to use a telescope to observe the planets, discovers the moons of Jupiter, the rings of Saturn, and the phases of Venus.

1758 Halley's Comet returns as predicted by Edmond Halley, proving that earlier observations of comets in 1531, 1607, and 1682 were, in fact, sightings of the same comet, which completes an orbit of the sun every 75 years or so.

1781 William Herschel discovers the planet Uranus.

1801 Giuseppe Piazzi discovers the first asteroid, Ceres, which is now considered a dwarf planet.

1838 Friedrich Wilhelm Bessel measures the parallax of star 61 Cygni.

1846 The planet Neptune is discovered after both British and French teams of astronomers begin looking for a planet beyond Uranus.

1930 Clyde Tombaugh discovers the planet Pluto.

1957

The Soviet Union launches Sputnik, the world's first artificial satellite, marking the start of the Space Age.

1958 The United States launches its first satellite and forms NASA.

1962 The Mariner 2 becomes the first unmanned craft to successfully visit another planet when it passes near Venus.

1966 The Venera 3 becomes the first unmanned craft to land on another planet, Venus.

1969

Apollo II Astronauts Neil Armstrong and Buzz Aldrin land on the moon.

1971 The Mars 3 Lander is the first unmanned craft to land on Mars.

1974 The Mariner 10 spacecraft performs the first flyby observations of Mercury.

1977 The Voyager 1 spacecraft is launched to study the outer planets, passing Jupiter in 1979, and Saturn in 1980.

1986 The Voyager 2, also launched in 1977, flies close to Uranus and discovers 10 of its moons.

1989 Voyager 2 flies close to Neptune and Triton, one of its moons.

2005 The discover of the dwarf planet Eris is announced by the team of Mike Brown, Chad Trujillo, and David Rabinowitz.

2006 Pluto is reclassifed as a dwarf planet.

Introduction

Have you ever stared up at the stars at night and wondered how they got there? Have you looked at the moon and wished you could land on it and explore its surface? Do you dream of being an astronaut and walking on the face of another planet? Do you think of being an astronomer, and examining the planets with telescopes? Maybe you could drive a robotic rover over the landscape of a foreign world, by remote control.

You know that the solar system is made up of planets, moons, and other objects, but do you know how we learned about them? We know about the solar system because scientists, astronomers, and astronauts have spent many, many years studying the sky, and developing more and more advanced tools to study it, including telescopes, rockets, probes, and rovers. Their efforts have gained much information about our neighboring planets in the solar system, as well as taught us about our own planet and the life and environment on it.

This book will help you learn about the planets and other objects that make up the solar system, and some astronomical objects beyond it. The book is divided into three sections. The first section, **What is the Solar System**, describes the solar system and what we know about its components. The second section, **Astronomy & Exploration Tools**, covers the history of human study of space and the solar system, and the tools we used to do it. The third section, **Beyond the Solar System**, investigates the history of the universe, and things in space that are beyond our solar system.

Most of the projects in this book can be made by kids with minimal adult supervision, and the supplies needed are either common household items or easily available at craft stores. So take a step toward the planets and get ready to **Build it Yourself**.

Spotlight on Famous Astronomers

Tycho Brahe (1546–1601) was a Danish nobleman, and one of the most interesting characters in the history of astronomy. He discovered a supernova in 1572. His careful observations of the motions of the planets allowed his assistant, Johannes Kepler, to devise his rules of planetary motion.

Caroline Lucretia Herschel (1750–1848) was a German astronomer living in England. She worked closely with her brother William Herschel and helped him with his discovery of the planet Uranus. She also discovered three nebulae and eight comets on her own. She was the first woman to discover a comet.

Henrietta Swan Leavitt (1868–1921) began her career at the Harvard College Observatory and worked her way up to director of stellar photometry, which measures the intensity of a star's radiation. Leavitt discovered Cepheid variables. These are stars that brighten and dim in a steady pattern related to their size. She developed a formula that described this relationship. This allowed her, and astronomers who came after her, to calculate the distance of these stars.

S. Jocelyn Bell Burnell (born 1943) is an astrophysicist from Northern Ireland. She was the first person to discover a pulsar in 1967 while she was a graduate student at the University of Cambridge. She discovered it with her teacher, Antony Hewish. Hewish later received the Nobel Prize for this discovery, though many people think that Burnell should have shared the prize.

Edwin Hubble (1889–1953) spent his entire career at the Mount Wilson Observatory in California, where he made some fascinating discoveries. He used the Hooker Telescope at Mount Wilson to detect Cepheid variable stars in the Andromeda Nebula. This proved that Andromeda was not just a cloud of gas, but was its own galaxy, a collection of billions of stars two million light years from ours. He also discovered that the other galaxies in the universe are all moving away from each other, and that the universe itself is expanding. This gave support to the Big Bang Theory of the creation of the universe. He helped us understand that we live in a huge universe full of billions of galaxies, each with billions of stars. The Hubble Space Telescope was named in his honor.

Percival Lowell (1855–1916) was an American businessman and world traveler from a wealthy family in Boston. He built the Lowell Observatory in Flagstaff, Arizona, to pursue his interest in Mars. Lowell also believed that there was a planet beyond Neptune, and spent the last years of his life looking for it. Fourteen years after his death, a young man name Clyde Tombaugh discovered this planet, Pluto, while working at the Lowell Observatory.

Clyde Tombaugh (1906–1997) built his own telescope and made drawings of Jupiter and Mars based on his observations. He sent these drawings to the Lowell Observatory in Arizona. His drawings were so good that, even though he had no formal training in astronomy at this point, he was offered a job at the observatory. While there, he was assigned to look for a mysterious planet "X" that was believed to lie beyond Neptune. Percival Lowell believed such a planet was responsible for disturbances in Neptune's orbit. Tombaugh discovered this by looking carefully at pictures of the sky from one night to the next, looking for any points of light that moved as much as such a planet should. He found one in 1930, which turned out to be Pluto. He went on to study astronomy formally, even though he had already discovered a planet. Tombaugh discovered 14 asteroids, some of which he named after his wife and children.

What is the Solar System?

VERY PERSON YOU KNOW AND EVERY PLACE YOU HAVE EVER been is located within a very small segment of the **universe** called the **solar system.** The solar system is actually quite big compared to you, your backyard, or even the whole earth itself, but it is tiny compared to the size of our **galaxy,** and minuscule compared to the entire universe.

So what is the solar system? What is it that separates the solar system from the rest of the universe? What makes it a system of connected parts? Most simply, it is defined by the sun and its **gravity.** The solar system is named after Sol, our sun. The rest of the solar system is all of the **planets, asteroids, comets,** and **meteors** that are held in orbit around the sun by its gravitational pull, as well as the **moons** and rings that orbit the planets. Everything held in place around the sun by its gravity is part of the solar system.

Words to Know

universe: everything that exists everywhere.

solar system: the sun with the celestial bodies that orbit it.

celestial bodies: planets, moons, asteroids, comets, stars, and galaxies.

galaxy: a collection of star systems.

gravity: the force that pulls all objects with mass towards each other.

planets: large celestial bodies that orbit around the sun.

asteroids: rocky objects that orbit the sun and that are smaller than the major planets.

comets: balls of ice and dust that orbit the sun.

meteors: the streak of light when a small bit of rock or ice, from an asteroid or comet, enters the earth's atmosphere.

moon: a celestial body orbiting a larger planet.

Milky Way Galaxy: the galaxy in which the solar system is located.

atmosphere: the air or gas surrounding a planet.

THE SUN IS A NUCLEAR FURNACE

The sun is a star, only one of hundreds of billions of stars in the **Milky Way Galaxy.** We already know that hundreds of these stars have their own planets around them, so our solar system may only be one of millions or billions of star systems. Additionally, our galaxy is only one of billions of galaxies in the universe. Let's take a tour of our solar system. We'll start at the sun, which is not only located in the center of the solar system, but is also the reason the

The Terrestrial Planets

Mercury is the smallest of the four terrestrial planets and is closest to the sun. Venus comes next, but is actually hotter than Mercury because its heavy atmosphere traps heat. Neither Mercury nor Venus has moons. Next in order is the earth and its moon, Luna. Finally comes Mars, and its two moons, Deimos and Phobos.

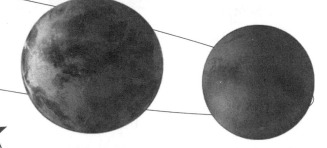

THE TERRESTRIAL PLANETS:
MERCURY, VENUS, EARTH AND MARS

system is a system and not just a bunch of separate things adrift in space. The sun is a huge **nuclear** furnace, fusing **hydrogen** into **helium**. This **fusion reaction** creates a lot of energy, which is the light and heat that we see and feel on Earth. Of course, if the sun didn't exist, we wouldn't either, because it's also the source of the light energy that plants turn into food.

The fusion reactions take place inside the sun, thousands of miles deep, and at temperatures of millions of degrees. The energy produced makes its way to the surface of the sun to escape as sunlight. While the surface of the sun is much cooler than the **core**, it is still about 6,000 degrees Celsius, more than hot enough to melt any material, such as steel or human beings, on its surface and turn it into a gas.

Words to Know

nuclear: relating to the nucleus of an atom.

atom: the smallest particle of matter.

hydrogen: the most common element in the universe, and one of the elements of water.

element: a pure substance that cannot be broken down into a simpler substance, and contains only one type of atom.

helium: the second most common element in the universe.

fusion reaction: produces the energy output of the sun when hydrogen nuclei react to form helium.

core: deep inside; the center.

terrestrial planets: Mercury, Venus, Earth, and Mars.

DID YOU KNOW?

MARS LOOKS RED BECAUSE THERE IS A LOT OF IRON OXIDE ON THE SURFACE—THIS MEANS MARS IS BASICALLY COVERED IN RUST!

The Terrestrial Planets

Moving away from the sun, we first encounter the four **terrestrial planets.** Terrestrial means "earth-like" and, in order, these are Mercury, Venus, Earth, and Mars. These planets may not seem very earth-like. Mercury and Venus are much, much hotter than the earth, and Mars is much colder. Humans could not breathe on any of them, and as far as we know so far, there is no liquid water or life on any of them. However, the four terrestrial planets do share some things in common. They are all balls of rock mostly made of silicate materials (rocks made of silicon and oxygen), and **iron.** They are also roughly the same size, compared to the much larger planets beyond Mars.

Past Mars we reach the asteroid belt. Asteroids are irregular, rocky balls smaller than planets that also orbit the sun. They are found throughout the solar system, but most of them are collected in certain places. Hundreds of thousands of them are located in the asteroid belt, an area between Mars and Jupiter. Astronomers used to speculate that these might have been the remains of an early planet that was ripped apart by

the gravitational pull of Jupiter. Now most suspect that the gravity of Jupiter kept the planet from ever forming.

The Jovian Planets

Past the asteroid belt we reach Jupiter, the first and greatest of the four **Jovian planets.** These are also called the gas giants because they are many times the size of earth and are made of gas, mostly hydrogen and helium. The name "gas giants" though, may not be a very accurate name, because even though the surface that we can see is made of gases, most of the mass of these planets may be liquid. "Liquid giants" might be a better name. It's also possible that any of the Jovian planets may have a rocky core, like a terrestrial

★ Words to Know

iron: an element that is a common metal.

Jovian planets: Jupiter, Saturn, Uranus, Neptune.

Dwarf Planets

In the middle of the asteroid belt there is a dwarf planet called Ceres. It is the largest of the asteroids, and it is also the first of what are called "dwarf planets" or minor planets. A dwarf planet is big enough to have been pulled into a round shape by its own gravity. It orbits the sun, rather than orbiting another planet, like the moon. However, unlike the eight large, or major planets, it doesn't dominate its orbit. Ceres is only one of thousands of asteroids in the belt, and is only a little bit larger than some of the others.

planet at its center, beneath thousands of miles of gas and liquid. Scientists haven't figured that out yet.

Jupiter is the largest of the gas giants, and is also the second largest object in the solar system, second only to the sun itself. In fact, the solar system has been described as the sun, Jupiter, and some debris, because the sun and Jupiter make up 99 percent of the total mass of the solar system. The earth and all the other planets only make up a very small amount of the total mass. Jupiter has over three hundred times the mass of the earth, and is more than three times as massive as the next largest gas giant, Saturn.

Jupiter has its own weather patterns, which are visible in the colorful lines and stripes in its atmosphere. Most noticeable of these patterns is the Great Red Spot, an incredibly large storm that has circled like a hurricane in the atmosphere of Jupiter for hundreds of years. Beneath the atmosphere of Jupiter the gas becomes dense enough to change into a liquid. Jupiter is mostly an ocean of liquid hydrogen. It also has faint rings around it, but these are not as large or as visible as the rings of Saturn.

DID YOU KNOW?

JUPITER HAS 63 MOONS, THE LARGEST NUMBER OF MOONS OF ALL THE PLANETS IN THE SOLAR SYSTEM. THESE INCLUDE IO, EUROPA, GANYMEDE, AND CALLISTO.

VENUS

MARS

MERCURY

EARTH

JUPITER

Measuring Distance in Space

The planets in our solar system are really far away from each other! The distance from the sun to the earth is called an Astronomical Unit, or an AU. From the sun to Jupiter is over five times the distance from the sun to the earth, or 5 AU. You would have to travel almost that same distance again to reach Saturn. One has to go quite far past Saturn to reach Uranus and Neptune. Uranus is 20 AU from the sun. Neptune is another 10 times the distance from the sun to the earth past Uranus, or 30 AU from the sun.

Furthermore, it also has two large clouds of asteroids, the Trojan and Greek asteroids, which travel around the sun ahead of, and behind Jupiter.

Saturn is the next planet after Jupiter, and is famous for its large, colorful rings, which are visible from Earth with only a basic telescope. These rings are made up of thousands and thousands of small particles, a few feet across on average, in orbit around Saturn. These rings are estimated to be about 700 feet thick, but they appear very thin in comparison to their width. They are about 200,000 miles across. It is because of this great size that they appear to be flat and solid, when they are actually not solid at all, but made up of small parts with empty space between them. Saturn is also orbited by 60 moons, including its largest, named Titan.

URANUS

Once past Saturn, the solar system seems quite empty for some distance. There is a scattering of tiny **planetoids,** called Centaurs, between Jupiter and Neptune. But there are so few of these, they are so small, and the planetoids are spread over so large a distance that we are unlikely to bump into them on our way from Saturn to the next planets.

Uranus and Neptune are similar in

★ Words to Know

planetoid: a small celestial body resembling a planet.

axis of rotation: an imaginary line through a planet's poles, around which it rotates.

elliptical: shaped like an ellipse, or an oval.

many ways to each other. In fact, they are sometimes called the "ice giants" as opposed to the "gas giants" of Jupiter and Saturn, because they are so cold that much of their mass may actually be frozen. They are close in size to each other, about 30,000 miles in diameter, and are both around 15 times as massive as the earth, though Neptune is slightly denser, and thus more massive than Uranus. Both have small rings of fine particles that are easily observable from Earth. They also have many moons: Uranus has 27, and Neptune has 13.

One unique thing about Uranus is that it is tipped on its side. Its **axis of rotation**, around which it spins, is facing toward and away from the sun, rather than up and down at (roughly) a right angle from the plane of its orbit, like the earth and most of the other planets. The result of this is that the North Pole of Uranus has daylight for 42 years, and then night for 42 years. Some astronomers think that Uranus was knocked on its side by a

collision with another celestial body in the early years of the solar system.

Neptune's atmosphere appears blue, with streaks of white clouds, though these are not clouds of water like those on Earth. Its atmosphere changes rapidly, and has had a number of "Great Dark Spots" appear and disappear in it. These are storms similar to Jupiter's Great Red Spot.

The Kuiper Belt and Beyond

Past Neptune the solar system gets relatively crowded again, as the edge of the Kuiper Belt begins here, and extends to as far as 100 AU. One AU is 93 million miles. The Kuiper Belt is similar to the asteroid belt and contains tens of thousands of asteroid-like icy objects, called Kuiper Belt Objects, or KBOs. Two of these KBOs are big enough to be considered dwarf planets. These are Pluto and Eris.

NEPTUNE

Pluto was the first of the Kuiper Belt Objects discovered, and is relatively close to the sun compared to the other objects. Its orbit is **elliptical** so it sometimes comes much closer to the sun. Sometimes it is even closer to the sun than Neptune. For a long time Pluto was counted as the ninth planet in our solar system but recently scientists decided that it really is only a dwarf planet. Pluto also has three moons, named Charon, Nix, and Hydra. Eris is slightly larger than Pluto and is farther out. Its orbit can take it more then twice as far out as Pluto. It also has its own moon, Dysnomia.

So far, the farthest object from the sun that is still part of the solar system that we have observed is an object named Sedna. It may be a Kuiper Belt Object, but it travels far beyond the Kuiper Belt, to over 880 AU. This is really far! It is 880 times 93 million. All of these things past Neptune are called trans-Neptunian objects, or TNOs.

We've reached the end of the tour of the solar system. However, one of the great things about science is that it is always revising itself as more information is discovered. So, by the time you are reading this, more dwarf planets may have been discovered, or more moons of the gas giants may have been found. Maybe you'll grow up to make an important discovery about the solar system yourself!

PLUTO

The Oort Cloud & Comets

At the very edge of our solar system lies the Oort Cloud. This is a cloud of comets, or more specifically, the dusty, icy balls that, when they fall toward the sun, we see as comets. The Oort Cloud might reach as far out as 50,000 AU and is believed to be the source of long-period comets. These are comets that take thousands of years or more to travel around the sun. Because there is little direct evidence for its existence, the Oort Cloud remains just an idea, at this point. But it makes sense as a source for comets.

Short-period comets are ones like Halley's comet that orbit much closer to the sun. They are visible from the earth much more frequently. In the case of Halley's comet, this is once about every 77 years. These comets may have begun in the Oort Cloud, but they were knocked out of the cloud by the pushing and pulling of the gravitational field of other members of the cloud. Then they were pulled into a closer orbit to the sun by the gravity of the other planets.

Past the Oort Cloud we leave the solar system, and move out to the rest of our home galaxy, the Milky Way.

How BIG Is Space?

SPACE IS HUMONGOUS. WHEN WE MEASURE THINGS ON Earth, we can use units like feet, meters, and miles. But outer space is so big that in order to talk easily about the distances between objects in space we use larger units of measurement than those we use every day. One of these larger units is the **Astronomical Unit**.

An Astronomical Unit, abbreviated AU, is the average distance between the sun and the earth. This is about 93 million miles. That is a very large distance to try to imagine. If you could drive a car to the sun, driving 24 hours a day at 60 miles an hour, it would take you over 176 years to get there.

The word astronomical comes from the word astronomy, which is the study of the solar system and outer space. Astronomical means related to the science of astronomy, but it also means huge, vast, or inconceivably large.

93 MILLION MILES= 1 AU

MAKE YOUR OWN
SCALE MODEL OF AN

1 First you'll make a model of the sun. Cover your workspace with sheets of newspaper. Inflate your beach ball or balloon. Mix the water and flour in a large bowl to make a papier-mâché paste. Tear some newspaper into strips, and them dip in the paste. Lay the strips of paper on the beach ball, covering the entire ball in a few layers, except for a small area around the nozzle of the ball. Let it dry overnight, or over several days if necessary.

2 Take your small pea or bead, and using your blue and green paints, paint it like the earth. Some craft stores even sell beads that already look like the earth. Don't worry too much about matching the shape of the continents. This is a very small model. Glue your pea or bead earth model to the top of one of your sticks.

3 Once your sun model is dry, paint it yellow like the sun. (Don't look directly at the sun for a model, though!) Let the paint dry. Once the paint is dry, you can deflate

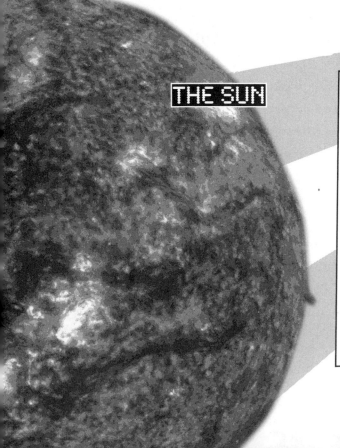

THE SUN

SUPPLIES

* I beach ball or extra-large round balloon, 2 feet in diameter
* 3 cups flour
* 6 cups warm water
* large bowl
* newspaper
* I pea or bead, I/4 inch in diameter.
* small paintbrush
* paint—yellow, blue, and green.
* 2 dowels or long sticks, about 3 feet long
* glue and tape
* large field, like a football or soccer field

ASTRONOMICAL UNIT

EARTH

the ball or balloon at the spot you left uncovered. Attach the sun to the top of the other stick. You can push your stick or dowel through this hole in the bottom of the sun.

4 Go outside to the large field. If it is a football field, push the dowel with the sun model into the field at one of the goal lines. You might want to do this to the side of the field on the sidelines, so your dowels don't go in the field itself. Check with the person in charge of the field first to make sure it's okay to stick the dowel in the field. If not, you can fill a bucket with sand and stick the dowel in the bucket, then place the bucket at the goal line.

5 Take the stick with the earth on it, and place it halfway between the 28th and 29th yardline, on the opposite side of the field. This will put 71.5 yards between the earth and sun models. If you are at a soccer field, this is a little more complicated, because the size of soccer fields can

vary. If your field is 110 meters long, place your sun at one penalty box, and your earth at the other. This will give you roughly the same distance. If you don't have either a football or soccer field marked out, you can measure the distance with a measuring tape. You need a total distance of 244 feet 6 inches, or 74.5 meters between your sun and earth.

6 Standing next to your earth model, look at the sun model. Now imagine that your pea (or bead) is two billion times its size, or about the size of the earth. If the pea were the size of the earth, and your sun model were the size of the sun, and the distance between the earth model and the sun model were increased by the same amount, that would be one Astronomical Unit. Now look away from the sun model, and imagine a point forty times that distance from the sun, past the earth. That point, on the scale of your model, would be almost two miles away. So when we say that Pluto is 40 AU away from the sun, that is the kind of distance we are talking about.

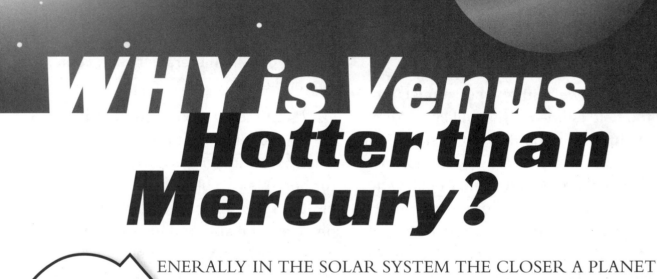

WHY is Venus Hotter than Mercury?

CENERALLY IN THE SOLAR SYSTEM THE CLOSER A PLANET is to the sun, the hotter it is, and the farther away it is, the colder it is. So Mars is colder than Earth, and Pluto is much, much colder than either of them. There is one important exception to this—the surface temperature of Venus is much hotter than Mercury, even though Venus is about twice as far from the sun as Mercury is. The reason for this is that Venus has a thick atmosphere of what are called "greenhouse gases," mostly carbon dioxide (CO_2), while Mercury has very little atmosphere at all. These gases in Venus's atmosphere allow visible light from the sun to warm its surface, but block infra-red light bounced off of the surface from leaving the

CARBON DIOXIDE

atmosphere. Greenhouse gases are very important. If the earth did not have some in its atmosphere, the earth would be much colder than it is now.

Your can make a greenhouse that will create a similar process to what happens on Venus. Even though Venus receives less sunlight than Mercury, it keeps more of the heat. Greenhouse gases in the atmosphere of Venus, Earth, and other planets don't work exactly the same way as your greenhouse. But the plastic wrap of your greenhouse keeps hot air from rising and taking away the heat. This is called **convection.** Greenhouse gases, like on Venus, block the escape of heat in the form of infra-red light, called **radiation.** Both allow energy in, in one form, and block it from leaving, in another.

Now, as far as we know, no plants or any forms of life live on Mercury or Venus. Both are so hot that there is no liquid water on either planet. But by growing plants in your boxes, you can see how important the greenhouse effect is on the earth.

★ Words to Know

convection: the transfer of heat from one region to another by the movement of a gas or liquid.

radiation: the process by which energy like light or sound moves from its source and radiates outward.

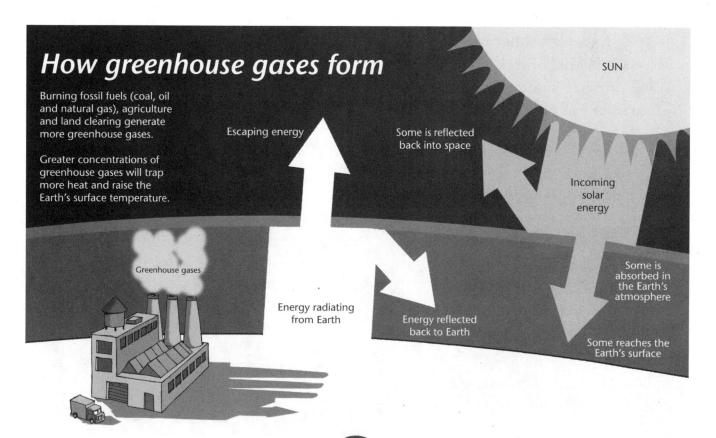

How greenhouse gases form

Burning fossil fuels (coal, oil and natural gas), agriculture and land clearing generate more greenhouse gases.

Greater concentrations of greenhouse gases will trap more heat and raise the Earth's surface temperature.

SUN

Escaping energy

Some is reflected back into space

Incoming solar energy

Greenhouse gases

Energy radiating from Earth

Energy reflected back to Earth

Some is absorbed in the Earth's atmosphere

Some reaches the Earth's surface

MAKE YOUR OWN GRE

1 Fill the pots with potting soil. Plant the seeds and water according to the directions on the packet.

2 Place the pots inside the shoeboxes. Label one of the boxes "Mercury" and place a thermometer inside. This is what is known in experiments as a "control." If you want to see the effect of something, in this case a greenhouse, you have to be able to compare it to how the situation would be without that thing.

3 Label the other box "Venus" and place the other thermometer inside. Tape four sticks in the corners of this box, sticking straight up about a foot.

4 Tape one end of the plastic wrap to the top of one side of the shoe box, and then wrap around the top of the stick frame you built. Tape down the plastic wrap on the other side of the box. Do the same thing on the other two ends of the box. The plastic wrap forms a greenhouse around your pot.

5 Place both boxes outside in the sun. After about 10 minutes, look at the thermometers and compare the two temperatures. Both should have received the same amount of sunlight, but one of them should be warmer than the other.

Venus Mercury

SUPPLIES

- 2 small pots
- dirt or potting soil
- seeds for plants that grow well in warm or hot weather
- 2 shoeboxes
- pen or pencil
- 2 thermometers
- 4 sticks or dowels about a foot long
- tape
- plastic wrap

ENHOUSE EXPERIMENT

6 Let the seeds grow, watered and cared for as the seed packet instructs. Make sure that whatever you do for one plant, you do for the other. Water them the same amount, and if you give one plant food, give the same amount to the other. We want the greenhouse to be the only difference between the two. Scientists have a fancy term for this. It's called isolating the independent variable. Measure the difference between the growth of the two plants. If you planted flowers, count the number of flowers. Compare the height of the plants, and count the number of leaves. Take measurements at least once a week and write down the measurements and the temperature of each box.

Rings Around the Planets

SATURN IS SURROUNDED BY HUGE RINGS. THEY EXTEND 60,000 miles and look like large, flat disks, but they are actually not solid at all. Instead, they are made up of millions of much smaller pieces orbiting Saturn. Some are as large as a house, but most are much smaller, many are even as small as grains of dust. Many of these pieces are also covered with ice. They reflect the sun's light. From a distance, all these small pieces together appear to be solid.

While Saturn can be seen by the naked eye, it appears to be just a bright point of light. When people (such as Galileo) first looked at it through telescopes, they saw Saturn's rings for the first time. But it was unclear with these early telescopes what these rings were. They seemed to change size and shape, from almost round to elongated. The rings even appeared to disappear at times. They are beautiful colors, including pinks, blue-gray, and sandy browns.

You can make a model of Saturn's rings yourself, and see how the rings can appear to change shape.

MAKE YOUR OWN
PLANETARY RINGS MODEL

1 Place the dowel or pencil through the center of the disk so that it pokes out an inch or so on the other side. Use some clay to make it fit tightly.

2 Hold the stick in one hand and gently spin the disk like a top. While spinning, apply a small amount of glue to one point on the disk. Keep the bottle of glue still, and spin the disk, so that you make an even ring of glue.

3 Sprinkle your powder onto the ring of glue while carefully spinning the disk. You can use different colors for different sections of the ring. Look for dirt that is the color of Saturn's rings, or you can use food coloring to dye sugar different colors. Blow off the excess powder that hasn't stuck to the glue. Let the glue dry.

SUPPLIES

* dowel or pencil
* clear plastic disk with a hole in the middle*
* piece of clay
* glue
* powder—dirt, sand, **flour**, sugar, or even glitter
* clay ball that you can cut in half, 1^1/$_2$ inches in diameter**
* dark room and **flashlight**

* You can use template A to cut a disk out of a clear piece of plastic, like a plastic plate. You can also use one of the clear plastic disks that are placed on the top of a spindle of blank CDs or DVDs.

** You can also make a papier-mâché ball by blowing up a small balloon to about 1^1/$_2$ inches in diameter, and covering it with papier-mâché. See Make Your own Model of an Astronomical Unit on page 10.

4 Repeat steps two and three as many times as you would like, to create many different rings. You can use different-colored powders to make different-colored rings. Make sure that you blow off the excess, and let the glue dry between each repetition. If you want your model to be a model of Saturn, **use the template** as a guide for placing your rings.

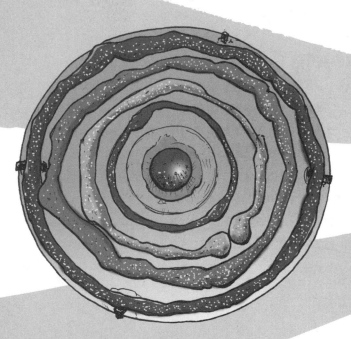

5 Remove the stick from the center of the disk. Glue one half of your ball on top of the disk in the center above the hole, and the other half of your ball to the bottom of the disk. If you are making a model of Saturn, you might want to paint it to look like Saturn. See the illustration on page 7 for ideas.

6 Mount your model on a stick, or hang it from a string. Turn off the lights and shine a flashlight on your model from across the room. Now you will see how a large amount of small particles can look solid from a distance, like Saturn's rings. Notice that if you look at the model from straight on the edge, the rings nearly disappear. Remember, Saturn's rings are much thinner compared to the size of Saturn than the rings on your model are compared to your Saturn. Tilt the model slightly. As you tilt it, the rings look larger. This is the same with Saturn when viewed from the earth.

DID YOU KNOW?

ALL FOUR OF THE JOVIAN PLANETS—JUPITER, SATURN, URANUS AND NEPTUNE HAVE RINGS AROUND THEM. SATURN'S ARE JUST THE BIGGEST AND MOST NOTICEABLE.

Phases of the Moon

THE MOON GOES THROUGH PHASES, IN WHICH IT appears to change shape. It goes through these changes over the course of a month. In fact, the reason we count time in months is based on these changes of the moon. The moon appears to get bigger **(wax)** and get smaller **(wane)** even though the moon stays the same shape and size. This is really an illusion caused by the change in the positions of the earth, the moon, and the sun, and the light reflected from the moon.

Even though we talk about "moonlight," and the moon "shining," the moon doesn't actually create any light of its own. All the moonlight we see is really just sunlight reflected by the moon.

★ Words to Know

wax: get bigger.

wane: get smaller.

crater: round pit in the moon or other celestial body caused by the impact of a meteorite.

mare: dark area on the moon of solidified lava. From the Latin for "sea," the plural is maria.

MAKE YOUR OWN
PHASES OF THE

1 Make a model of the moon by blowing up a round balloon, and covering it with papier-mâché. The moon is about one-fourth the diameter of the earth, so you should make your moon model about a fourth of the diameter of your globe. For example, if your globe is 16 inches in diameter, (a common size) then your moon should be about four inches across. When the papier-mâché dries, paint the model to look like the moon. Paint it white, and then add in **craters** and dark areas, called **"maria."**

2 Wrap one end of a coat hanger into a small loop around the base of the globe. Bend the rest of the coat hanger into an "L" shape. Mount the moon model on the other end of the coat hanger. Note that your model will not be to scale in terms of the distance between the moon and the earth. To make this distance to scale for a 16-inch globe, your coat hanger would need to be about 37 feet long!

3 Mount your flashlight or desk lamp on a stable surface so that it shines on your moon model. You might have to tape the light in place. Make sure that the light can shine over or past the globe and illuminate your moon. This light represents the sun, though the real sun would be many times larger than the earth and moon and would be much farther away.

DID YOU KNOW?
THE DARK SPOTS THAT MAKE UP THE FACE OF THE "MAN IN THE MOON" ARE CREATED BY THE DIFFERENCE IN THE REFLECTION OF SUNLIGHT BETWEEN THE MARIA AND THE HIGHLANDS. OTHER CULTURES SEE THESE SPOTS AS FORMING OTHER IMAGES, SUCH AS A RABBIT OR A FROG.

MOON MODEL

4 Turn on your light and turn off all the other lights in the room. (If you are doing this in a room with windows, you might have to close the shades or wait until night time.) Now stand with your back to the light, and move your globe and the moon model so that the light shines on the globe. Rotate the moon around the globe, and see how the shape of the moon appears to change based on the position of the moon in relation to the earth and the sun.

SUPPLIES

* globe
* balloon
* papier-mâché
* white and black paint
* wire coat hanger
* tape
* **fl**ashlight or other light source that can be aimed—a dome desk lamp or reading lamp that shines light in just one direction will work

ORBITING
Moon Model

TO UNDERSTAND THE STRUCTURE OF THE SOLAR system, one needs to understand **orbits.** Planets, asteroids, and comets orbit around the sun. Moons orbit around planets. Our moon, Luna, orbits the earth, and dozens of moons orbit Jupiter. So what is an orbit? Why do things travel in orbits?

An object stays in orbit because of forces working upon it. **Newton's** first law of motion says that an object will travel in a straight line until something acts on it, by pushing or pulling it off of a straight line. The forces that are acting on planets and moons to keep them in orbit are gravity and **momentum.**

The gravity of two objects pulls them together, according to Newton. But, according to **Einstein**, the mass of the two objects actually bends space and time, so a planet or star creates a "**gravity well**" that an orbiting planet or moon falls into. In Newton's model, gravity pulls two objects towards each other through empty space, as if they were connected by invisible ropes. In Einstein's model, space isn't empty, but is a material that is shaped by the mass of an object. In this model, objects fall towards each other because they are trapped in the bending of space caused by their masses. At the same time, the planet or moon has a great deal of momentum that keeps it circling around the larger body, which keeps it from falling into the larger body, at least for a while.

If a body has too much momentum, it may orbit the larger body a few times, and then escape the gravity well, continuing on past the larger body. If the gravity and momentum match just right, however, the smaller body will enter a stable orbit around the larger body, circling it for a long time.

DID YOU KNOW?

WHEN METEOROIDS, SMALL PARTICLES OF DUST AND ROCK IN THE SOLAR SYSTEM, HAVE TOO LITTLE MOMENTUM, THEY CAN FALL INTO THE EARTH'S ATMOSPHERE, BURNING UP AND BECOMING METEORS. IF PART OF THE ROCK SURVIVES TO LAND ON EARTH, IT IS CALLED A METEORITE.

★ *Words to Know*

orbit: the path in space an object makes as it revolves around another object.

Newton: Sir Isaac Newton (1643–1727), an English physicist and mathematician who discovered laws of motion and gravity.

momentum: the force that a moving object has in the direction that it is moving.

Einstein: Albert Einstein (1879–1955), a German/Swiss/American physicist who created the theory of relativity.

gravity well: the distortion in the fabric of space-time created by the mass of an object, and into which other objects fall.

meteoroid: a meteor revolving around the sun.

MAKE A MODEL OF THE
ORBIT OF THE

1 Cut the plastic bag apart so you have one large sheet of plastic. Pinch the center of the bag and tie a rubber band around it.

2 Fill the plastic bottle with water or sand and tie it around the pinched center of the bag. Place the bottle in the center of the cardboard box.

SUPPLIES

* black plastic trash bag
* scissors
* rubber band
* small plastic bottle
* water or sand
* string
* large cardboard box
* globe
* tape
* stick, about 1 foot long
* ball, about 3 inches in diameter

3 Pull the plastic sheet around the edges of the cardboard box. Pull it tight so that the bottle pulls the center of the sheet down into the center. This plastic sheet represents the fabric of space and time and the center is the gravity well created by the mass of the earth.

4 Place the globe in the center of the plastic sheet, in its "gravity well." Tape the stick to the top of the globe. Wrap a few layers of tape around the top of the stick, a half an inch or so down from the top.

5 Tie a loose loop in one end of the string and place it around the stick, resting on top of the tape. It should be loose enough to rotate easily around the stick, but not enough to slide down past the tape.

6 Attach the other end of the string to the ball, leaving enough length for the ball to roll along inside the gravity well. (If your model were to scale, however, the string would have to be 30 feet long.)

MOON AROUND THE EARTH

7 Swing the moon around the earth. See how many times you can get it to orbit the earth. Your moon will only orbit a few times because it doesn't have the momentum of the real moon. Momentum is determined by how big something is, and how fast it is going. Also, the friction of the ball on the plastic and the string around the stick will slow down the ball. Still, this is a good example of how gravity and momentum work to create orbits.

CENTER

Geocentrism & Heliocentrism

HAVE YOU EVER SEEN THE EARTH MOVE? IT'S HARD TO
see, because you're standing on the earth as it moves. Have you
seen the sun move? It sure looks like the sun is moving as it rises in
the east in the morning and sets in the west in the evening. Common sense would suggest that the sun travels around the earth,
and that the earth stands still. For many years, people believed
that   this was the case. One of the beauties and wonders of science,
however, is that sometimes it proves that what "common sense" tells us is true
is actually false.

From the earth, it does look as if all the planets and the moon
and the sun are traveling in orbit around us. But things got a little

Earth Centered or Sun Centered?

One of the great debates in the history of science was about whether the sun and the planets revolved around the earth, or whether the earth and the other planets revolved around the sun. The first theory is called "Geocentrism," ("Geo" means earth, so Geocentric means "earth centered") and the second is called "Heliocentrism." ("Helio" means sun, so Heliocentric means "sun centered.")

complicated when trying to figure out the motion of the planets. Sometimes it looked as if the planets were moving backwards in their orbits. This is called "retrograde motion." Ptolemy, an early astronomer, accounted for this motion by speculating that the planets were mounted on invisible, crystal spheres, that spun as they revolved around the earth. Thus, when the planets appeared to move backwards, they were rotating away from us on their spheres. Then, Ptolemy could predict where the planets would be based on the speed that the spheres rotated, and the speed at which they revolved around the earth.

However, other astronomers thought that the earth and the other planets moved around the sun. Copernicus made a rival Heliocentric model of the solar system that could predict the movements of the planets just as well as Ptolemy's. His model still had the planets moving in perfect circles and still rotating in spheres, but he placed the sun in the center.

Another astronomer, Johannes Kepler, using observations of his own and his mentor, Tycho Brahe, improved on Copernicus' model by realizing that the planets don't revolve around the sun in perfect circles, but in fact revolve in **ellipses**. This accounted for the apparent retrograde motion of the other planets, and meant that Kepler could get rid of the invisible crystal spheres of Ptolemy.

★ Words to Know

geocentrism: the belief, now disproved, that the earth is the center of the solar system.

heliocentrism: The belief that the sun is the center of the solar system.

ellipse: a regular, oval-shaped geometric figure.

MAKE YOUR OWN
GEOCENTRIC AND

1 Lay out your two big pieces of cardboard, and label one "Geocentric" and the other "Heliocentric." On the one labeled Geocentric, mount a marble or ball in the center of the board on top of a tall stick, at least a foot tall, and label it "Earth."

2 Cut out two small circles of cardboard, and mount them on the top and bottom of a short stick, two or three inches tall, making a dumbbell shape. Stand the stick on one circle, the base, and glue a marble to the edge of the top circle. These will represent the planets. You can make more detailed models out of papier-mâché and paint them to look like the planets if you wish. This circle represents the sphere that the planet rotates around inside. Label this one "Moon." Tie a short length of string to the stick, loosely enough so that the circle can rotate within the loop of string. Tie the other end to the stick marked "Earth" on your Geocentric model.

3 Repeat step 2 six more times, but each time make the stick slightly taller, and the string a little longer, so that the strings from the planets further from the earth can pass over the closer ones. Label the planets in this order, going out from the earth: Mercury, Venus, Mars, the sun, Jupiter, and Saturn. (The ancients did not know about Uranus and Neptune yet.) Pull each stick away from the earth until its string is taut. Now you can move the planets along their circular orbits, and spin them in their "spheres."

4 Now, on the other piece of cardboard marked "Heliocentric," place a ball on a

SUPPLIES

* cardboard, 2 big pieces and several smaller pieces
* markers or paint
* 16 marbles and/or small balls
* sticks (pencils, straws, chopsticks, long matchsticks, or skewers)
* glue
* tape
* scissors
* string

HELIOCENTRIC MODELS

stick representing the sun a little off center. Place another stick (with nothing on top) a few inches away from the sun. These two points are the focus points of the ellipse.

5 Make another set of planets on sticks and bases and label them—Mercury, Venus, Mars, Jupiter, and Saturn. Unlike the first set, these don't need a big circle, or "sphere" on top. Just put the planet on top of the stick. (Kepler's model doesn't need the spheres to explain retrograde motion.) Make the ones closer in to the sun shorter than the ones farther away.

6 Make a stick on a base with a circle on top. In the center of the circle, place the earth, and on the outside of the circle, place the moon. The moon is the one object in the Heliocentric model that does orbit the earth. Make this piece taller than the one for Venus, but shorter than the one for Mars.

7 Tie one end of a string to the sun, wrap the string once around the stick on your Mercury model, and tie the other end around the other focus point. Now, pull Mercury away from the focus points until the line is taut, and move the planet in orbit around the points. This will create an elliptical orbit around the sun.

8 Repeat step 7 five more times in this order: Venus, Earth, Mars, Jupiter and Saturn. Make each string longer than the previous one.

Compare your two models. Which one do you think is simpler? Both models explained the movements of the planets equally well for a number of years, but one needed the addition of the invisible spheres. A guide that scientists sometimes use for deciding which of two competing models explains things better is called "Occam's Razor." This is named for a thinker named William of Occam, who said that things don't become more complicated without a reason. This suggests (though it doesn't prove) that if two different models explain something equally well, the simpler one is probably right, and is the one we should go with until more evidence to support one or the other model can be found.

What Makes a Comet's Tail?

A COMET IS A "DUSTY SNOWBALL," A BALL OF FROZEN WATER and methane ice, mixed in with some dirt and dust. Many thousands of such balls are believed to orbit the sun, many of them far beyond the outer planets in a group called the "Oort Cloud." This cloud is named after an astronomer, Jan Oort, and may extend as far away from the sun as 50,000 AU. Other comets may come from a closer band of objects called the Kuiper Belt.

Astronomers think that some comets may get bumped out of the Kuiper Belt or the Oort Cloud by the gravitational pushing and pulling of the other comets, at which point they fall into an orbit that takes them closer to the sun, and the earth. When these comets get closer to the sun, we see them better because the light reflected off of them is less diffuse, and because they "grow" a tail from the **solar wind**.

What, then, is the solar wind? In addition to the light it gives off, the sun also constantly shoots out a mass of electrically charged particles, mostly hydrogen and helium atoms, which is called the solar wind. These are a result of the nuclear reactions taking place inside the sun. (It really isn't a wind like we have on Earth, though, as the wind on Earth is caused by hot and cold air moving around, while there is no air in space. Further, the solar wind only "blows" in one direction—away from the sun.)

When the solar wind hits a comet, something exciting happens. The particles knock some bits of ice and dust off the comet, which stream out behind the comet as it flies along, making a "tail." The sunlight then reflects off the tail, making it visible to us.

You can model this effect.

DID YOU KNOW?

HISTORICALLY, SOME PEOPLE BELIEVED COMETS TO BE SIGNS OF BAD THINGS TO COME, LIKE WARS, FAMINES, OR PLAGUES. WE NOW KNOW THAT THESE ARE NOT CONNECTED, AND THE APPEARANCE OF A COMET IN THE SKY IS NOTHING TO BE AFRAID OF. IF A COMET ACTUALLY WERE TO HIT THE EARTH, HOWEVER, THAT MIGHT BE A DIFFERENT STORY. WHEN A SMALL PIECE OF A COMET HIT THE EARTH'S ATMOSPHERE NEAR TUNGUSKA, RUSSIA, IN 1908, THE EXPLOSION BLEW DOWN ABOUT 80 MILLION TREES.

Words to Know

solar wind: the stream of electrically charged particles emitted by the sun.

sublimation: to change from a solid to a gas, or from a gas to a solid, without being a liquid in between.

The Auroras

When the solar wind hits the earth's magnetic field near the North or South Poles, the electrically charged particles react with the magnetic field, giving off waves of light called the aurora borealis or northern lights and the aurora australis or southern lights. You may have seen these one night if you live or visit far enough north or south.

MAKE YOUR OWN SOLAR WIND MODEL

1 Place the fan and saucer on a table or counter in your dark room, and position them so that the fan is blowing across the top of the saucer. The fan will represent the solar wind.

2 Put the dry ice in the saucer. Important: Never touch dry ice directly with your skin. It is much colder than regular ice, and can quickly give you frostbite. (Frostbite is what happens when the water inside your body's cells freezes. This can cause permanent damage and is very painful.) Use the heavy gloves or tongs to move it.

3 Pour some water on the dry ice and into the saucer. Turn on the fan. Turn out the lights in the room and turn on the flashlight. Aim the flashlight directly at the dry ice and the tail of vapor that is flowing out behind it. See how the block of ice has now "grown" a tail.

SUPPLIES

* electric fan
* shallow saucer or container
* a dark room
* dry ice
* tongs or heavy gloves
* water
* flashlight

32

CRATER
Maker

I F YOU LOOK AT THE MOON THROUGH A TELESCOPE, YOU CAN SEE marks, or craters, on its surface. Most rocky planets and moons in the solar system have craters. Even the earth has lots of craters, but they are harder to see because of erosion caused by wind and water. What makes those craters?

There are two sources of craters. Some are impact craters. When an object, like a comet or meteor, slams into a moon or planet, it leaves a hole in the surface. This is a crater. There might even be a visible meteor crater somewhere in your area.

Volcanic activity can also create craters. This happens when hot gases and molten rock (called magma) in a volcano are under so much pressure that it bursts through the surface of the planet. Not all planets and moons are volcanically active. If a planet or moon appears to have volcanic craters, which look different from impact craters, this may suggest that the planet had molten magma under its surface at some time in the past. Look at pictures of the moon and other cratered bodies in the solar system. What types of craters do you see? Do any of them appear to have been volcanically active?

You can model both types of craters.

MAKE YOUR OWN CRATERS

1 Cut a small hole in the side of the box, big enough to slide in one of your straws or plastic tubes. Push a straw through the hole, keeping the bendy end on the outside of the box. Bend the end of the straw so it points up. Crimp the end of another straw and slide it into the end of the first straw inside the box. Bend the end of the second straw so that it points upward inside the box. Tape the straws where they join down to the bottom of the box.

2 Fill the box with sand or dirt almost to the top. Cover over the end of the straw inside. If the straw pokes up too high, cut it down shorter to below the level of the sand. Lay a thin layer of a different color of sand or dirt on top of the first one.

3 Tie your rubber bands in a line, by folding one around another and then slipping it back inside itself.

4 Tie one end of your rubber tubing or line of rubber bands to one end of your forked stick, and tie the other end to the other fork. You have now made an old-fashioned slingshot that kids have played with for generations. Important: Do not fire anything out of your slingshot at any person or animal, or at anything breakable. It's best to fire it outside only. Don't take it to school, either. Remember that science should be used only for good, not evil.

SUPPLIES

* low **flat** box, like the lid from a box of copier paper
* scissors
* bendy drinking straws or plastic tubing
* tape
* fine dirt or sand, in two different colors
* heavy rubber bands or rubber tubing
* thick, forked stick
* pebbles

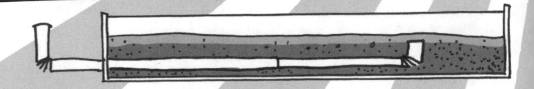

5 To make a volcanic crater, blow hard and fast through the straw or tube. Your breath represents the exploding gases escaping from under the surface of the planet.

6 To make an impact crater, place a pebble in the middle of the rubber band of your slingshot, pull it back, and fire it out of your slingshot. Practice a couple of times before you fire a pebble into the sand in your box. Experiment with different angles of impact, and different size pebbles. See how the lower color of dirt gets exposed, and see how the crater is shaped. Look at how different the two types of craters appear. The moon has been hit by thousands of impacts over the years, and has craters on top of craters. Shoot pebbles on the edges of other craters and see how the impacts overlap.

Bonus activity: Make your own photo of the "moon."

If you have access to a digital camera, take a closeup photograph of your crater box. Carefully pick out any pebbles in the middle of the craters if you can without disturbing the craters or leaving finger marks. (The real meteors that cause lunar craters are often destroyed by the impact, though some craters will have small piles of rubble in the center that are the remains of the impactor.) Upload your picture to a computer with a photo-editing program. Make sure to ask your parents first if you are using their computer or camera. Use the photo-editing program to make your picture of the crater box look as much like the moon as possible. Crop out the edges of the cardboard box, and change the color to black and white. Experiment with the other filters and tools and see if you can get it to look as much like pictures of the moon as possible. Then you can print it out. See if you can get anyone to think it is really the moon. If you succeed, let them know, gently, that you made it yourself.

Asteroid Belt

IN THE SOLAR SYSTEM, BETWEEN MARS AND JUPITER, IS A LARGE group of asteroids. Asteroids are small, rocky objects that orbit the sun. Many of the asteroids in the solar system are grouped together in the space between Mars and Jupiter. Because they orbit the sun in a rough ring, they are referred to as the "asteroid belt."

Some astronomers have speculated that these asteroids might have been part of a planet that had formed in an orbit here, and that the planet was torn apart by the gravitational pull of Jupiter. Others think that the gravity of Jupiter may have prevented these asteroids from ever forming into a planet in the first place. This hypothetical planet, which may or may not have existed, has a name. It is called Phaeton.

Words to Know

accretion: the process by which larger bodies are created from the attraction of smaller bodies.

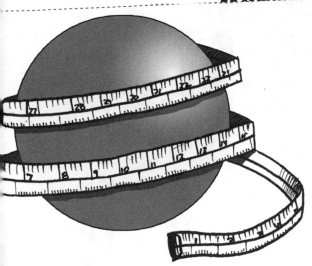

Big Enough to Be Round

One definition of a planet is a body that orbits the sun that is also big enough to be round. There are thousands of objects orbiting the sun, of all sizes and shapes. Most of these asteroids and comets have irregular shapes, like peanuts or potatoes. These bodies were formed by a process called **accretion**. Bits and particles of matter are attracted to each other by gravity, and slam into each other. Some of these stick together, becoming larger and larger. An asteroid could be formed by thousands of these collisions.

Once enough of these collisions occur, and the asteroid becomes big enough, the force of its own gravity will pull the mass of the body into a round shape. The exact size necessary depends on the composition of the body and exactly what minerals and elements it is made of.

Some astronomers don't care for this definition of a planet. Why? Because it means that small bodies, such as Pluto, Ceres, and Eris, now called "dwarf planets," would be called planets because they are big enough to be round.

Ceres

Ceres is the largest of the asteroids—almost 600 miles across. It is big enough that its gravity has made it round. It was discovered in 1801 and was considered a planet for a number of years. In keeping with the tradition of naming planets after Greek and Roman gods, it was named after the goddess of grain. Ceres is where the word "cereal" comes from, because cereal is made from grain, like corn or wheat.

DID YOU KNOW?

THE WORD "ASTEROID" MEANS "STAR-LIKE." WHEN PEOPLE FIRST SAW ASTEROIDS, THEY WERE THOUGHT TO BE LIKE LITTLE STARS, BECAUSE OF THEIR REFLECTED LIGHT. NOW WE KNOW THEY AREN'T VERY MUCH LIKE STARS AT ALL, BUT THE NAME STUCK.

MAKE YOUR OWN ASTEROID "BELT"

1 Attach the strip of fabric to the belt buckle. Depending on the design of the buckle, you might have to cut a small slit lengthwise in the end of the buckle. Or fold one end of the strip of fabric over the metal ring on the back of the belt buckle if there is a ring.

2 Sew the strip of fabric closed around the part of the belt buckle. Wrap the belt around your waist and mark where some holes in the belt should be so you can buckle it comfortably. Remove the belt and punch holes where you placed your marks.

3 Lay sheets of newspaper on a flat surface. Lay the belt out on top of the newspaper. Place many small drops of glue on the belt. Sprinkle the small pebbles or glitter or sequins on the glue and let them dry.

4 Put a drop of glue the size of your big pebble on the belt. Glue your big pebble or sequin there and label it "Ceres."

5 Label some of the other bits of glitter on the belt after some of the other asteroids. The next asteroids discovered were Pallas, Juno, Vesta, Astraea, Hebe, Iris, Flora, Metis, Hygiea, Parthenope, Victoria, Egeria, Irene, and Eunomia, and they were all considered planets until 1852. There are thousands of other asteroids as well.

SUPPLIES

* old belt buckle
* strip of black fabric 2 inches wide, long enough to go around your waist, plus about another 8 inches or so
* needle and thread
* marker that will show up on the black fabric
* punch awl or other tool for poking a hole in the fabric
* old newspaper
* glue
* tiny pebbles, glitter, or sequins
* 1 bigger, round pebble

MAKE YOUR OWN
PHAETON-ASTEROID
JIGSAW PUZZLE

1 Glue a sheet of white paper to a piece of cardboard. Let it dry. Place your plate on the paper and trace a circle around the plate with the pencil. Cut the circle out of your cardboard. This represents the planet Phaeton.

2 Paint or color the surface of the paper to look like a planet. Phaeton would have been a rock ball, like the terrestrial planets of Mercury, Venus, Mars, and Earth, or the moon. You can make it colorful, like Mars, and add craters like those on the moon.

3 Once your paint has dried, flip the planet over and draw lines dividing the planet into jigsaw pieces. You can use your imagination to design the pieces. Or, you can lay out another jigsaw puzzle on top of the planet, and then trace around its pieces, pulling them away one at a time and tracing the outlines of each piece as you remove them.

4 Carefully cut out the pieces. Assemble (and then disassemble) the pieces. When you take your Phaeton puzzle apart, this simulates the gravity of Jupiter ripping the planet into the asteroids we know today. When you put the puzzle together, you are simulating accretion, the process by which Phaeton and all the other planets were created. This occurs when particles such as atoms, gas, dust, rocks, asteroids, and even larger objects are pulled together by their gravity, creating larger and larger bodies like our earth and the other planets.

SUPPLIES

* cardboard
* white paper
* glue
* plate or other large, flat, round object smaller in diameter than your piece of paper
* pencil
* scissors
* colored markers, pencils, or paint

Volcanism

HEN A PLANET HAS MOLTEN ROCK UNDER ITS surface, it can sometimes cause geological activity like erupting volcanoes. **Volcanism** is an important factor in geology (and ares-ology, the "geology" of Mars) and the geology of other planets. We live on the solid crust of the earth. Beneath the crust lies the **mantle**, then the outer core and the inner core.

The inner core is believed to be solid iron, while the outer core is molten iron, and the mantle is solid rock. This outer core is molten because of the great heat within the earth. This heat comes from a few sources. Some is left over from the earth still cooling down from the impacts of the accretion that formed the earth. Other heat comes from the decay of radio-active elements—uranium, thorium, and potassium—that occur naturally in the earth. As these atoms decay, they give off heat and energy.

These sources of heat combined together are hot enough to melt rock. Even though the earth appears solid, much of it is actually liquid. This liquid rock in the mantle is called **magma**. Sometimes, when the pressure and heat of the mantle gets great enough, it bursts through the surface of the planet, the crust, forming a volcano. When the hot magma reaches the surface it is now called lava.

Volcanism is not limited to just the earth. Mars had many volcanoes in the past, but it seems to have cooled down enough to not currently have active volcanoes. Even some of the moons in the solar system have volcanoes. For example, one of Jupiter's moons, Io, has active volcanoes. One of them, the Tunshtav Volcano, spews hot particles over the surface of Io, covering an area as large as the state of Texas.

Tectonic Plates

What we think of as the solid earth is actually a thin, brittle crust floating on molten rock. This crust is further divided into pieces called tectonic plates. These plates move slowly over many millions of years. In some places they run into each other, creating mountains like the Himalayas in Asia. In others the plates are moving apart. For example, the two plates that North America and Europe sit on are moving apart at about two inches a year.

★ Words to Know

volcanism: the motion of molten rock under a planet's surface, which results in volcanos.

mantle: the layer of the earth between the crust and the core, the upper portion of which is partially molten.

magma: molten rock beneath or in the crust of the earth.

tectonic plates: large sections of the earth's crust, that move on top of the layer, the mantle, beneath.

MAKE YOUR OWN MODEL OF THE
TECTONIC PLATES
& VOLCANISM

SUPPLIES

* pudding
* a pot
* stove
* granulated sugar
* kitchen torch

1 Make pudding, either from a cookbook recipe or from a package. Place the pudding in a pot on the stove. Don't turn on the stove yet.

2 Sprinkle a coating of granulated sugar on top of the pudding. Use the kitchen torch to melt the sugar on top of the pudding. Move the flame quickly over the sugar and then move on. You want to quickly melt the sugar, and then let it cool, forming a hard crust on top of the pudding. This is similar to a French dessert called crème brulee, which means "burnt cream."

3 Gently heat up the pudding and watch what happens. The crust of sugar represents the earth's crust, while the hot pudding represents the hot mantle. The crust should break into pieces, and move about, like the tectonic plates, and bubbles of hot pudding may burst through the surface, like hot magma. **Be careful**, hot sugar or pudding can burn you!

4 Let the pudding and sugar cool again, and eat it.

Warning: Make sure you have adult supervision using the stove and torch.

DID YOU KNOW?

THE LARGEST MOUNTAIN ON MARS, OLYMPUS MONS, IS AN EXTINCT VOLCANO. OLYMPUS MONS IS THREE TIMES AS TALL AS MOUNT EVEREST ON EARTH.

ASTRONOMY &
Exploration Tools

OW DO WE KNOW ALL THAT WE KNOW ABOUT THE solar system? People have studied the structure and history of the solar system for thousands of years. How we have learned about the solar system is a fascinating history itself.

The earliest astronomical tools were simply our eyes. Many ancient civilizations carefully studied the sun, the moon, and the stars, and accurately described and predicted their movements across the sky. The Mesopotamians, Chinese, Aztecs and Maya, Egyptians, Druids, Greeks and Romans, and many others all paid careful attention to the movements of the heavens.

These early observers gathered some good data, but some of their assumptions based on that information were flawed. Sometimes science confirms common sense, but it can reveal that common sense is just wrong. The way things appear to be at first may not be how they actually are.

Heliocentrism vs Geocentrism

For example, when you go outside in the morning, it appears that the sun rises in the east. During the day, the sun appears to travel overhead and set in the west. For many years, people assumed that the sun (and the moon, planets, and stars) revolved around the earth. We have already learned about geocentrism, meaning "earth centered." This is not a bad assumption based on the information they had, it just happens to be wrong.

Another example of such an assumption involves the planets. When you go outside at night and look at the stars, some of the bright lights you see are not actually stars, but are in fact five of the planets. Mercury, Venus, Mars, Jupiter, and Saturn reflect enough sunlight to Earth that they can be seen with the naked eye. Because they look very much like the stars, early astronomers assumed that they were. The only thing that they could observe that distinguished these stars from all the others was that their movement through the sky was different from that of the other stars. They moved irregularly, even appearing to move backward at times. Because of this irregular movement, they were called the wandering stars. The word "planet" means "wanderer" in ancient Greek.

Mars

Planets and Their Names

Because the Roman Empire conquered England, our English names for the planets come from the names of the planets in Latin, the language of the Romans. The Romans, as the Greeks had done before them, named the planets after some of their gods. Mercury, Hermes to the Greeks, was the messenger god. Because the planet Mercury is closest to the sun, and thus has the shortest distance to cover in its orbit, (think of the inside track of a raceway) it moves most quickly across the sky. This makes it appropriate for a fleet-footed messenger. Venus, Aphrodite in Greek, was the goddess of beauty, while Mars (Ares), was the god of war. The association of the planet Mars with a war god was because of the blood-red color of the light that reflects off of its red-colored sand. Jupiter (Zeus), the largest planet, was named after the king of the Roman gods. Saturn (Cronos) was his father.

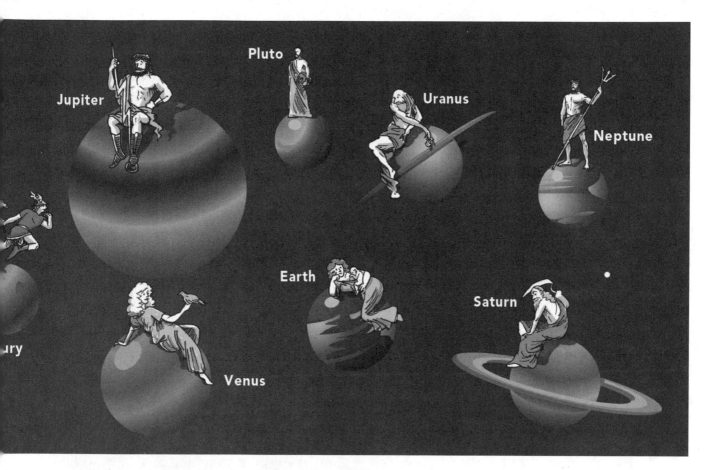

DID YOU KNOW?

ENGLAND HAD ITS OWN PRE-ROMAN ASTRONOMICAL TRADITION. THE STONEHENGE MONUMENT IS BELIEVED TO BE AN ANCIENT ASTRONOMICAL OBSERVATORY THAT WAS BUILT OVER FOUR THOUSAND YEARS AGO.

Our modern knowledge of the solar system really begins long ago with **Nicolas Copernicus (1473–1543)**. He was a Polish philosopher and politician who questioned the geocentric model of the solar system. About 1400 years earlier, Ptolemy, a Greek astronomer working out of Alexandria, Egypt, had developed a complicated model of the planets that could predict all of their movements. To account for their backward movement, he decided that the planets were spinning in invisible crystal spheres. Ptolemy calculated the exact speed that the spheres had to rotate and orbit the earth in order to accurately predict the movements of the planets in the sky.

Copernicus, however, thought that it was equally possible that the earth and the planets orbited around the sun. He calculated the speeds at which the spheres had to move to explain the motion of the planets in a helio-centric, meaning "sun-centered," model. These two competing models of the solar system explained the solar system equally well. Until better observations could be made, no one could be sure which model worked best.

Tycho Brahe (1546–1601), a Danish nobleman, realized that the dispute could only be resolved by gathering more accurate obser-vations. He built an observatory on the island of Hveen where he spent over 25 years making careful, precise observations of the movements of the stars. He designed a device called a quadrant that allowed him to measure the angle between a star and two other points. Brahe realized that neither Ptolemy nor Copernicus had ful-ly explained the movements of the plan-ets. Therefore, he created a compromise system, called the Tychonic, that had the other planets orbiting the sun, but the sun orbiting the earth.

Johannes Kepler (1571–1630), a German astronomer who was Tycho Bra-he's assistant, realized that if the planets' orbits around the sun were ellipses instead of perfect circles, he could account for all of the motion of the planets without rely-ing on crystal spheres at all. His new mod-el was superior in that it was simpler. This didn't prove it was right, but it suggested that it was on the right track. As a general rule, simpler explanations are more likely to be right. When an explanation requires the invention of things like invisible crystal spheres that should cause you to be suspi-cious.

Galileo Galilei (1564–1642) was an Italian astronomer who introduced the telescope to astronomy. Until then, tele-scopes or spyglasses had been used only to look at things on the earth, such as sailing ships coming over the horizon. This was one of the giant break-throughs in the science of astronomy. Galileo discovered that the planets were not stars, but were worlds like the earth. He also saw that Saturn has rings, the sun has sunspots, and the moon has craters.

Galileo also observed that Jupiter had its own moons revolving around it. This was the first proof that not everything in the universe revolves around the earth. While this suggested that other things might not revolve around the earth either, it didn't conclusively prove heliocentrism.

It took almost 200 more years for **Friedrich Bessel,** a German mathematician and astronomer, to finally prove heliocentrism once and for all. By this time, most astronomers had assumed this model was correct, but there was a race to prove it correct by measuring the first stellar **parallax**. Thousands of years earlier, the ancient philosopher Aristotle had reasoned that if the earth moves around the sun, the stars would look different from one side of the sun to the other.

For example, hold your arm out in front of you with one finger pointing up. Close one eye and look at an object in the distance, such as a tree or a building. Move your head to the right. Your finger (the closer star) will look like it is to the left of the tree (a distant star.) Move your head to the left, and the finger will appear to move to the right. The finger is not moving, however, your eye (the earth) is moving.

Aristotle had not been able to see any parallax, so he had assumed that the earth was not moving. The problem was that the parallax is there, but the distances from the earth to the stars are so great compared to the distance the earth moves around the sun, that the parallax could not be observed with either Aristotle's eye, or Galileo's telescopes. It was only with greatly improved telescopes that Bessel was able to measure the parallax of the star 61 Cygni in 1838. Measuring the parallax of a star also allows us to calculate how far away a star is. Thus, 61 Cygni, sometimes called Bessel's Star, was the first star whose distance we know. It is about 11 light-years, or 60 trillion miles, away from the earth.

New Planets and Other Objects

In 1781, William Herschel, a British astronomer, discovered the first new planet, Uranus. He originally named it George's Planet, after King George III, the king of England at the time. In keeping with the tradition of the other planets being named

Words to Know

parallax: the apparent change in position of a star compared to the stars behind it, as viewed from one side of the earth's orbit around the sun and compared to the view from the other side, half a year later.

after the Greek and Roman gods, astronomers eventually agreed to name the planet after Uranus, the Greek god of the sky.

Herschel also discovered the first two of Uranus's moons. His son, John Herschel, named them after Titania and Oberon, the fairy queen and king from Shakespeare's play *A Midsummer's Night Dream*. All of the other moons of Uranus follow this tradition and are named after characters from the works of Shakespeare or Alexander Pope, another British writer.

By 1846, astronomers had noticed irregularities in the orbit of Uranus. This suggested that another planet existed beyond Uranus whose gravitational pull was slowing it down. Astronomers searched for this mystery planet, which was found on September 23, 1846. Both John Couch Adams of England and Urbain Le Verrier of France were given credit for the discovery of Neptune, though there is still historical debate about this. Neptune was named for the Roman god of the sea, (Poseidon in Greek) and its moons, such as Triton, are named for Greek sea gods and nymphs.

In 1930, the American astronomer Clyde Tombaugh discovered the planet Pluto (now classified a "dwarf planet"), while working at the Lowell Observatory. He was only 24 years old at the time. Pluto (Hades in Greek) was the Roman god of the underworld, who could make himself invisible. The name was suggested by an 11-year-old girl, Venetia Burney, who was interested in both mythology and astronomy. Tombaugh also liked the name because its first two letters were the initials of the founder of the Lowell Observatory, Percival Lowell. Its moons are named after mythical beings associated with Pluto. Charon was the boatman that ferried the dead to the underworld over the river Styx. Nix was the goddess of night and Charon's mother, and the Hydra was a mythical beast that guarded the gates to the underworld.

Rocketry and Space Exploration

The next huge technological leap in astronomy after the telescope was the development of rocketry in the twentieth century. Rockets were used to launch all sorts of scientific instruments (and some scientists) into space. In the second half of the twentieth century, there was a competition between the Soviet Union and the United States to show which country was technologically superior. This competition was called the "Space Race" and resulted in many important improvements in rocket technology and our knowledge of the solar system.

The first probe from the earth to land on another body in the solar system was the Soviet Union's Luna 2 probe in 1959. It crash landed on purpose on the moon, and on the way there also discovered the solar wind. The first mission to another planet was the Mariner 2 mission from the United States, which passed near Venus in 1962. In 1966, the Soviet Venera 3 probe was the first to enter Venus's atmosphere. These and later Venera and Mariner missions discovered much about the atmosphere and composition of Venus.

These were all unmanned probes, however. The Space Race's most high-profile competition involved putting humans into space. Yuri Gagarin, a Soviet, was the first human in space in 1961, and his country-woman, Valentina Tereshkova, became the first woman in space in 1963. In 1969, the first humans, United States citizens Neil Armstrong and Buzz Aldrin, landed on the moon. The American missions to the

DID YOU KNOW?

ASTRONOMERS HAVE NAMED ASTEROIDS AND OTHER BODIES AFTER ENTITIES FROM OTHER MYTHOLOGIES BESIDES THE GREEK AND ROMAN LEGENDS. FOR EXAMPLE, SEDNA IS NAMED FOR AN INUIT GODDESS, VARUNA FOR A HINDU GOD, AND QUAOAR IS A GOD OF THE TONGVA PEOPLE, A NATIVE AMERICAN GROUP. THESE ARE ALL TRANS-NEPTUNIAN OBJECTS.

moon, called the Apollo missions, gathered a lot of information about the moon, including samples of moon rocks that they brought back to Earth.

More recent advances in computers, robotics, and remote-control technology mean that we can send much more complex probes into space without sending humans along. This saves a lot of energy, because we don't have to launch people, and all the food and water they need to survive. Nor do we have to worry about getting them back to Earth.

Mars has received the most attention of all the other planets so far. The Mariner 4 flew by Mars in 1964. Since then, the Soviet Mars and Phobos probes and NASA's Viking landers have all visited Mars, as have several more landers and orbiters, including the European Space Agency's Mars Express Orbiter. At the beginning of this century, there were six spacecraft either in orbit around Mars or on its surface. Two of the most successful of these have been the Mars Exploration Rovers, Spirit and Opportunity. They have been driven by remote control around the surface of Mars for more years than they were originally designed. Both NASA and the European Space Agency have announced plans to send humans to Mars by 2025 or 2030.

Some of the best new tools for learning about the solar system were not sent to other planets, but are aboard satellites and

Dwarf Planets

In 2003, a team of astronomers in California, led by Mike Brown, discovered a Kuiper Belt Object bigger than Pluto. This object caused a big fight among astronomers. Some thought this should be a 10th planet. Others did not think it qualified to be a planet. But, others argued, if it is not a planet, then should Pluto be termed a planet? All this disagreement led to a new classification—dwarf planet. When the new object was called a dwarf planet, Pluto also became a dwarf planet, as did the asteroid Ceres. Because of all the strife it caused among astronomers, the new object was given the appropriate name of Eris, who was the goddess of discord or strife. Its moon is named Dysnomia, the daughter of Eris, which means "lawlessness."

DID YOU KNOW?

THE NEW HORIZONS SPACECRAFT ALSO CARRIES SOME OF THE ASHES OF THE ASTRONOMER CLYDE TOMBAUGH, WHO DIED IN 1997. SOME OF HIS REMAINS WILL VISIT PLUTO, THE DWARF PLANET THAT HE DISCOVERED.

space stations in orbit around the earth. For example, the Hubble Space Telescope is in orbit around the earth, which allows it to take much clearer pictures than earth-based scopes. The earth's atmosphere interferes with light entering it, so it is like viewing objects through a glass of water. Because the Hubble orbits above the atmosphere, it avoids the interference from the atmosphere, providing much clearer images of very distant objects. The Hubble has given us great images of the planets, and shown that the universe is full of billions and billions of galaxies.

Spacecraft have also visited the outer planets, most notably the Voyager probes and the Galileo Spacecraft. The Voyager probes were launched in 1977, and passed closely by the gas giants over the next dozen years before heading out of the solar system. Voyager 1 is now the man-made object most distant from the earth. The Galileo probe traveled through the asteroid belt, and then circled Jupiter, studying its moons and atmosphere. It was crashed into Jupiter at the end of its mission to avoid an accidental crash landing into one of Jupiter's moons, which might have contaminated the moon with bacteria from Earth.

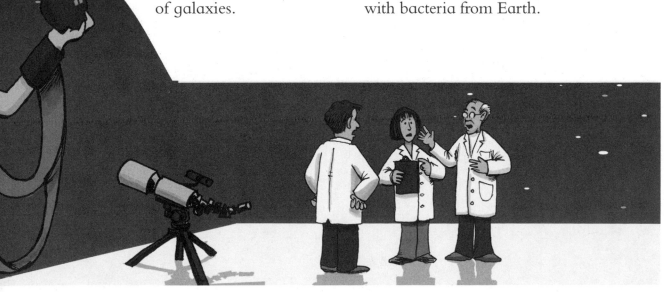

NASA's Deep Impact 2 probe launched an impactor into the Comet Tempel 1 in 2005 in order to study the material thrown up by the impact and learn about the composition of comets.

The New Horizons Spacecraft is on its way to visit Pluto, scheduled to reach it by the year 2015. Interestingly, it is powered by the radioactive decay of the element plutonium, which was named after the planet Pluto. Eight years after Herschel discovered Uranus, a German scientist named Martin Klaproth discovered the radioactive element uranium, which he named after Herschel's planet. In 1940, when scientists discovered two new elements, they were named neptunium and plutonium after the next two planets.

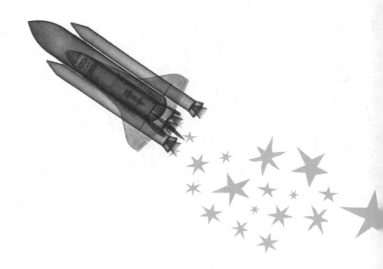

Galileo's Acceleration Ramp

IN ADDITION TO STUDYING THE PLANETS WITH A TELESCOPE AND discovering the moons of Jupiter and the rings of Saturn, Galileo did some experiments in motion. This is now called physics. One of the things he discovered was **acceleration**. When you peddle your bike harder, increasing your speed, you are accelerating.

However, Galileo discovered that when rolling balls down ramps, the balls speed up, even without anyone pushing them. The greater the angle of the ramp, the faster the balls accelerate. He was able to show that the rate at which the balls accelerate is constant. The fastest rate is achieved when the ramp is at a 90-degree angle to the ground—when the balls are dropped straight down. He also showed that it doesn't matter how big or heavy the balls are, they all accelerate at the same rate. This led to the story that Galileo dropped two different weights from the top of the Leaning Tower of Pisa. This may be an amusing story, but it most likely didn't happen.

Words to Know

acceleration: the process of increasing the speed of an object's movement.

MAKE YOUR OWN
GALILEO RAMP

1 Cut long, thin strips, about 1 inch wide, out of the cardboard, and tape it to the sides of the yardstick, making a trough.

2 Poke the tips of the pins through one side of the cardboard so that there is just enough room for the marble to roll past the pin, just nicking the tip, making a pinging sound. Repeat every two inches along the yardstick.

3 Prop up one end of the yardstick on a book or two, so that it is at a slight angle. With your watch in hand, roll the marble down the slope. Count the number of pings that you hear as the ball rolls down the slope. Notice how the pings become closer together as the ball approaches the end of the ramp. Now, looking at your watch, compare how many pings you hear in the first second with the number you hear in the second second. (You might need a friend to help you, with one of you counting pings and the other watching the clock.) The difference that you hear in the number of pings per second from the first to the second is acceleration.

4 Now experiment with changing the angle of the ramp by stacking more books under one end. The greater the angle, the greater the rate of acceleration.

SUPPLIES

* yardstick
* cardboard
* scissors
* tape
* pins
* marble
* books
* watch or clock with a second hand

Acceleration

Another scientist, Newton, later realized that the force that Galileo had measured in timing objects falling to the earth was the same force that caused the planets to orbit around the sun, and the moon to orbi the earth. This was one of the greatest scientific insights of all time. It was said that Newton figured this out when he saw an apple fall from a tree, while the moon hung in the sky behind the tree. People thought it made a better story to say that the apple hit him on the head.

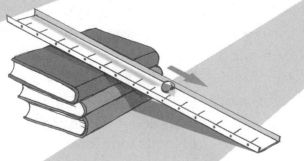

Galilean Telescope

A GALILEAN TELESCOPE IS NAMED AFTER GALILEO Galilei. He didn't invent this telescope though. Others, such as the Arabs and Dutch, already used these telescopes for viewing things on Earth from a far distance. For example, they were useful for looking from one sailing ship to another. Used like this, it is sometimes called a "spyglass." But Galileo was the first person to use this type of telescope for looking at the planets and the stars, so we call it by his name.

All optical telescopes work by focusing visible light. They focus distant light into a narrower beam so that you can see the light coming from objects that normally would be too spread out to see. A Galilean telescope uses two lenses to focus the light, while other kinds of telescopes use curved mirrors and lenses to focus the light.

MAKE YOUR OWN
GALILEAN

For this activity, you need to get your lenses together. You can cut fake lenses out of clear plastic, but they won't focus the light at all. Look around the house for an old pair of eyeglasses that no one needs. You can usually take the lenses out of eyeglasses by loosening the little screws on the sides of the frames. Alternately, you can use the lenses from a couple of magnifying glasses.

1 If you have one long cardboard tube, cut it in half. Take one of the two tubes and cut it lengthwise, on one side only. Now curl one side of the cut edge over the other side, so that this tube slides snuggly inside the other tube. Hold it at this size, take it out of the second tube, and tape it along its edge, so it keeps that size. Now place it most of the way back inside the other tube.

SUPPLIES

* long wrapping paper cardboard tube or 2 paper towel tubes
* scissors
* masking tape
* two lenses
* construction paper, paint, markers (optional)

2 Tape one lens to the outside of the larger end of your tubes. If your lens is from eye glasses, it will have a convex and concave side. The middle of the convex side bends outward, while the concave side bends inward. You can keep these terms straight by remembering that concave can fit things inside it, like a cave or cavity. Tape the lens so that the convex side faces the outside of the tube, and the concave side faces the inside. This lens is called the objective lens.

3 Tape the other lens to the outside of the inner tube. This is the eyepiece lens. Tape this lens with the convex side to the inside, and the concave to the outside.

TELESCOPE

4 If you want to decorate your telescope you can cover the larger tube with construction paper, and paint both tubes.

5 **Warning:** Do not look directly at the sun with (or without) your telescope. Look through the smaller end of the telescope, and aim your telescope at a faraway object, such as the moon. You can focus the telescope by moving the inner tube back and forth inside the larger one, to focus the image by bringing the lenses closer to, or farther away from each other. Since your telescope is really just a model, it may not help you see these objects much better. Why? Because for a telescope to work well, the lenses must be ground specifically for the distances at which it is intended to be used. Eyeglass lenses and magnifying lenses are just not designed for long distances. Try looking at something closer, like across the room.

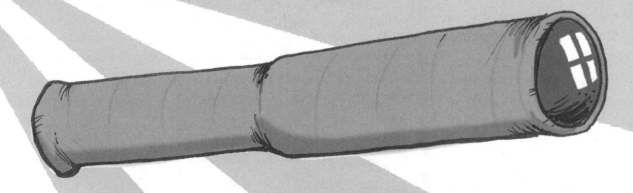

DID YOU KNOW?
THE S.A.L.T. (SOUTH AFRICAN LARGE TELESCOPE) HAS A MIRROR OVER 36 FEET ACROSS.

MAKE YOUR OWN
NEWTONIAN TELESCOPE

Can you make your own telescope that will work better? Sure. The easiest for an amateur to make is called a Newtonian telescope, and it uses a bent mirror to gather the light. You can build a basic one yourself. You can build an even better one with special equipment and adult assistance, which is beyond the scope of this book, but you can find sources in the resources section at the back of this book.

1 Remove one end from the cardboard box. Fill the tub or bowl with the clay or plaster. Let the plaster dry. Use sandpaper to smooth the plaster into a smooth, concave surface. Trace Template B in the back of the book onto cardboard, and use it to get the curve of your plaster just right.

SUPPLIES

* cardboard box or several sheets of **fl**at cardboard
* scissors
* large plastic tub or bowl
* clay or plaster
* sandpaper
* glue
* aluminum foil or silver mylar from a balloon
* I small mirror
* tape
* several long sticks

2 Cover the surface with a thin coat of glue, and then with aluminum or mylar foil. Be very careful to smooth out any wrinkles in the surface. This makes your reflector.

3 Position the bowl at the closed end of the cardboard box, with the concave surface facing the open end. Tape it securely in place.

4 Mount the small mirror on a stick and place it in the middle of the box, about I0 inches from the bowl, angled at a 45-degree angle.

5 Cut a small hole in the side of the box next to the small mirror. This should be positioned so that the light gathered by the reflector bounces off the mirror and through the hole.

6 Bring the box outside and brace it against a stable surface. Point the open end at an object, like the moon, and look through the hole in the side of the box.

Note that this is a very simple Newtonian telescope. You can make an even better quality one by grinding a glass reflector and having it "silvered." That means covered with a reflective material. However, this will require specialized equipment, as well as adult assistance. If you are interested, check the resources section for some websites and books that can get you started.

Rockets

THE ROCKET HAS BEEN AN EXTREMELY VALUABLE TOOL for space exploration. Satellites, unmanned probes, the Apollo missions to the moon, and even the Space Shuttle have all been launched by rockets. A rocket works by pushing gas out one end of the rocket, in the direction opposite the one we want the rocket to go. This works because, as Sir Isaac Newton discovered, for every action there is an equal and opposite reaction.

Our models will use pressurized air to provide the push. The second rocket is more powerful than the first one, and it should fly farther. If you enjoy making and launching these rockets, you might want to get into the hobby of model rocketry. These use burning fuel from manufactured engines to launch rockets. Some of these can go many hundreds or thousands of feet in the air. These require adult supervision, of course. You can find out more at your local hobby store, or there may be a model rocketry club in your area. Check out the resources section in the back of this book for more information.

Rocket Fuel

Rockets used for space exploration get the expanding gas for their power from burning fuel. Early rockets used burning gunpowder, while modern rockets use liquid oxygen and other fuels.

MAKE YOUR OWN MODELS OF
ROCKET MARK ONE

Caution: Always take care when launching any sort of rocket. Make sure you are in a wide open space, such as a park or big back yard. Make sure there is nothing breakable around, and let everyone in the area know what is about to happen.

1 Place the balloon inside the tube, with the open end sticking out the bottom. Put a drop of glue on the top of the balloon, and glue it to the inside of the tube near the top.

2 Cut three fins from construction paper and glue them to the sides of your tube near the bottom.

3 Cut a circle from construction paper, and then cut a triangle out of the circle, like cutting out a slice of pie. Fold the circle into a cone and glue it together. Glue this to the top of your tube, to make a nose cone.

4 Glue the straw to the side of the tube. Wait for all the glue to dry before going on.

SUPPLIES

* balloon
* cardboard tube from paper towels or toilet paper
* glue
* scissors
* construction paper
* straw
* straight stick or dowel thin enough to fit loosely in your straw

5 Place the stick in the ground, pointing straight up. Blow up the balloon so it is pushing against the inside of the tube. It's okay if some of the balloon is sticking out the bottom. Pinch the end of the balloon closed, but don't tie it off. Place the rocket onto the stick by sliding the straw down onto it.

6 When you are ready, release the end of the balloon. The escaping air should launch your rocket.

DID YOU KNOW?
THE CHINESE FIRST BUILT ROCKETS OVER TWO THOUSAND YEARS AGO.

AND
ROCKET MARK TWO

Caution: Always take care when launching rockets. Make sure you are in a wide open space, and that there is nothing breakable around. Let everyone in the area know what is about to happen. Have an adult help with the cutting.

1 Cut out fins and a nose cone from construction paper and glue them to the plastic bottle as you did in Rocket Mark One. The end of the bottle with the lid will be the bottom, so glue the nose cone to the opposite end. Glue the straw to the side of the bottle, as you did in Rocket Mark One.

2 Use the needle to punch a small hole in the bottle next to the lid. This is your exhaust port. Cut out a piece of the inner tube that includes the valve and about half an inch around the valve.

3 Use the craft knife or drill bit to cut a hole in the lid of the bottle big enough to fit the valve from the inner tube. Glue the piece of inner tube inside the cap so the valve sticks out.

SUPPLIES

* construction paper
* scissors
* glue
* empty plastic soda or water bottle, the taller and skinnier the better
* straw
* needle
* old bicycle inner tube that you can cut up
* craft knife or drill bit
* water
* stick that can fit loosely inside the straw
* bicycle air pump

4 Fill the bottle about a third to halfway with water. (You might have to experiment with several launches to get the ideal amount of water. Pay attention to how much you add each time.) Screw the cap on the bottle. Push the stick firmly in the ground, sticking straight up.

5 Attach the bicycle pump to the valve. Turn the bottle over, and slide it down on the stick, keeping your thumb on the exhaust port. Pump air into the bottle until it becomes too difficult to pump more in. You might need an assistant to pump while you hold the exhaust port closed.

6 Disconnect the bicycle pump from the valve. Remove your thumb from the exhaust port to launch the rocket.

SPUTNIK

ONE OF THE IMPORTANT MILESTONES IN THE HISTORY OF human exploration of the solar system was the launching of the first artificial **satellite**. A satellite is an object, like the moon, that orbits a planet. Today we have hundreds of artificial satellites in orbit around Earth and other planets like Mars. Some of these satellites are used for everyday things, such as broadcasting television signals and cellular phone calls. Others look for weather patterns on the earth, or communicate with global positioning devices like the one you might have in your car, that tell you where you are on Earth. Other satellites, however, contain scientific instruments, such as telescopes for observing the stars and other planets.

A country called the Soviet Union launched the first artificial satellite, named Sputnik, into orbit around the earth in 1957. That country no longer exists, but from 1922 until 1991 it included Russia, Ukraine, Belarus, and several other countries.

Words to Know

satellite: an object that orbits a larger object in space, whether natural or artificial.

MAKE YOUR OWN SPUTNIK

Your model will be a life-size replica of Sputnik. That's right, the first manmade satellite was that small, though the radio and other equipment inside made it weigh about 183 pounds. By comparison, the Hubble Space Telescope would weigh 12 tons on Earth.

1 Blow up the balloon until it is about 23 inches in diameter. Tie it off. Mix the water and flour together in the bowl to make papier mâché.

2 Tear the newspaper into strips, dip them into the flour and water mixture, and lay them over the balloon to make a sphere. Cover the balloon completely. Let it all dry.

3 Spread a thin film of glue over the sphere. Wrap the sphere in aluminum foil. Try to make the surface as smooth as possible. Trim off extra foil with scissors wherever it bunches up. Make a band of aluminum foil about two inches across around the center of the sphere.

4 Cut out four pieces of cardboard like template C at the end of this book. Fold them on the dotted lines so they form wedge shapes. Space the wedges evenly around the top of the sphere, with the open side facing downward.

SUPPLIES

* large round balloon or ball, 23 inches in diameter
* yardstick
* **flour**
* water
* large bowl
* glue
* newspaper
* aluminum foil
* scissors
* cardboard
* cardboard toilet paper tubes
* wire coat hangers
* clay

SATELLITE

5 Cut two toilet paper tubes in half. Cut them in half again length wise, and then roll them over top of themselves, taping them closed. You should now have four small tubes that can fit inside the openings of the wedges. Glue the tubes in place, sticking out of the wedges.

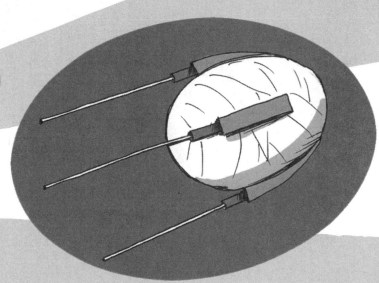

6 Unfold the coat hangers so that you have four straight pieces of wire. Insert them into the tubes so that they stick out the bottom of the tubes. Wedge them in place with the clay. These are the antennae of Sputnik which it used to broadcast radio signals to Earth. This is what Sputnik really looked like!

DID YOU KNOW?

THE WORLD'S LARGEST ARTIFICIAL SATELLITE IS THE INTERNATIONAL SPACE STATION. THE LARGEST NATURAL SATELLITE IS THE MOON, OF COURSE.

Balloon
Aerostat

BALLOONS HAVE BEEN USED FOR EXPLORING THE EARTH and other planets in our solar system. In France in 1783, the Montgolfier brothers launched the first hot air balloon to carry humans.

Some balloons have been used to lift scientific instruments into the earth's atmosphere to learn more about the layers of gases that compose it. Studying the atmosphere helps scientists understand the weather. Weather balloons carry instruments high into the atmosphere, including thermometers to measure temperature and barometers to measure air pressure.

In 1984, the Soviet space agency used balloons to lower instruments into the atmosphere of Venus as part of the Vega missions to Venus. A balloon used for taking such measurements is sometimes called an aerostat or an aerobot.

Venus Exploration

Sending balloon aerostats on rockets to Venus helped scientists discover that the gases in its atmosphere trapped sunlight, creating the greenhouse effect. This makes Venus warmer than Mercury, even though Mercury is closer to the sun and receives more total sunlight. It is one of many examples of how studying other planets has helped us learn more about our own.

MAKE YOUR OWN
AEROSTAT BALLOON

1 Poke four small holes in the sides of the box near the top. Tie small pieces of string through the holes, and then hang the box from the bottom of the helium balloon with the string. Tie one end of the remaining spool of kite string to the balloon.

2 Use the thermometer to record the temperature at ground level. Write it down on your paper.

3 Put the thermometer in the box, and let out the kite string so that the balloon rises as high as it can, while still holding on to the string. Let the balloon hang at the end of the string so that the thermometer will record the temperature at the higher elevation.

4 Pull the string in as quickly as you can, bringing down the balloon and thermometer. Quickly check the thermometer and see if the mercury in it is moving. If it is rising up toward the ground level temperature, this means it was cooler higher up in the sky. If it is dropping, this means it was warmer. Write down the temperature, and calculate the difference in temperature. There may or may not be any difference today, but try it on different days.

Balloons in Space

Other balloons were used in the early days of spaceflight to take humans as close to space as they could get without rockets or planes. The record for parachuting from the greatest height was not set from a plane, but from the Excelsior III balloon in 1960 by Captain Joseph Kittinger. He jumped from over 102,800 feet above the earth. This was an experiment to help learn how humans could survive re-entry from near space.

SUPPLIES

* small cardboard box
* scissors
* kite string
* helium balloon
* a thermometer
* paper and a pencil

The EAGLE Has Landed

THE LAUNCH OF SPUTNIK LEAD TO A COMPETITION BETWEEN the Soviet Union and the United States called the Space Race. It was a race to see who could reach certain goals in space first. The Soviets followed the success of Sputnik by putting Yuri Gagarin, the first man in space, in 1961, and Valentina Tereshkova, the first woman in space, in 1963. Shortly after the launch of Sputnik, the United States created NASA, the National Aeronautics and Space Administration, in 1958. NASA caught up with the Soviets, and won the race to put people on the moon in 1969.

The NASA program to explore the moon was called the Apollo program, and the 11th mission in this series landed Neil Armstrong and Buzz Aldrin, the first men to ever go to the moon. The earlier missions had tested the spaceships used, and orbited the moon without landing. The trip to the moon used two vehicles, a command module that stayed in orbit around the moon, which was commanded by a third astronaut, Michael Collins, and the moon lander.

MAKE YOUR OWN
EAGLE LANDER

The landers were called Lunar Modules, or LMs. Each Apollo mission had a different LM, and each had its own name. The LM-5, which was assigned to the Apollo II mission, was named the Eagle. You can make a model of the Eagle.

1 Take the cardboard box and cut four diagonal slits in the top and bottom of the box at the four corners, about a third of the way along each side. Cut one slit in each side connecting one of the pairs of top and bottom slits. You should now have four corners that are only connected at one side. Fold these into the box, and tape in place, creating an octagonal box.

SUPPLIES

* small cardboard box, about 6 inches across
* scissors
* tape
* glue
* gold mylar film from a ribbon or a mylar balloon
* straws
* 4 bottle caps
* toothpicks
* flat (not corrugated), white cardboard
* markers
* aluminum foil

2 Cover the box with the gold mylar film. Also cover four straws, four bottle caps, and three dozen toothpicks with the mylar. Do this by cutting thin strips of film, gluing the straw or stick, and then wrapping the strips around them.

3 To build the landing legs, cut a straw about six inches long. Glue one end to the middle of one of the bottle caps.

4 Cut two toothpicks in half. Glue two of these to the other end of the straw, then glue the other ends of the toothpicks to the top corners on the diagonal sides of the box. Glue two full-length toothpicks from the bottom two corners of the same diagonal side of the box, straight out to the straw. This will make the leg stick out at an angle. Glue two more toothpicks diagonally from the top of the straw to the bottom corners of the box.

DID YOU KNOW?

THE APOLLO MISSIONS PLACED REFLECTORS ON THE MOON. BY BOUNCING LASER BEAMS FROM THE EARTH OFF THESE REFLECTORS, AND THEN MEASURING THE TIME IT TAKES THE BEAM TO RETURN, ASTRONOMERS CAN PRECISELY MEASURE THE DISTANCE FROM THE EARTH TO THE MOON.

5 Repeat steps three and four three more times, adding three more legs to the box. Cut the remaining toothpicks in half, and glue ten of them horizontally along one of the legs to form a ladder. You have now finished the descent stage of the lunar module.

6 Carefully cut out a piece of cardboard to the shape of template D from the end of the book, and two pieces to the shape of template E. Fold along the dotted lines and glue in place. This makes the ascent stage. Cover the ascent pieces in aluminum foil. Glue the ascent module on top of the descent module.

7 With a black marker, draw two windows on the front. Also draw the ingress/egress port (the fancy NASA term for a door) above the ladder.

MAGNETIC Rail Launcher

BEFORE WE CAN SEND A SPACESHIP TO THE MOON, MARS OR anywhere else in the solar system, we have to get it off the earth. This takes a great deal of energy. Most of the energy used by a rocket to launch a spaceship is used to get the spaceship off of the earth. Much less energy is needed to push the ship toward its goal.

Traditionally, rockets have been used for getting objects into space, either to put them in orbit around the earth or to send them on to other parts of the solar system. There are other methods that could be used, including the magnetic rail launcher. Sometimes it's called a magnetic rail gun, but it doesn't shoot bullets, and you couldn't use it for hunting. Rather than having an object push itself with expanding gases, like a rocket, a rail gun pushes the object with magnetic force.

Science fiction writers, such as Arthur C. Clarke, the inventor of the **geosynchronous** satellite, thought these rail launchers could be used to launch spacecraft from the earth. Instead, we went with rockets. But, rail launchers may get a second look as a way to launch people and cargo from the moon or Mars once we set up permanent bases there. Both Mars and the moon have less gravity than the earth, so rail guns on either body would need less energy to launch things.

MAKE YOUR OWN
MODEL MAGNETIC

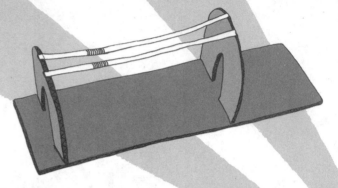

1 Cut the straw in half lengthwise. This will be your rail. Cut out two saddle-shaped cardboard supports, and tape them to either end of the rail. Put the rail on top of a large piece of cardboard and tape it in place.

2 Make an electro-magnet. Wrap wire around a nail as many times as it will fit. Tape one end of the wire to one end of a battery. Run the other end to a paper clip. Tape a second piece of wire from the other end of the battery to underneath the paper clip. Tape a piece of cardboard on the paper clip so that you can touch the clip—you are making a button. Bend the clip so that when you press down on the button, the circuit will connect, magnetizing the nail. Make two more electro-magnets just like the first.

3 Cut a small, straight piece of paper clip and place it on one end of your rail. Place one electromagnet underneath the rail at just the right distance so that when you connect the circuit, the piece of paper clip will be pulled toward the magnet. This may take some fiddling to get just right, so be patient.

4 Place the next two electromagnets under the rail at a similar distance down the rail so that when they are turned on, they pull the piece of paper clip farther down.

Words to Know

geosynchronous: orbiting the earth at the same speed at which the earth rotates, so that the object remains in place over the same spot on the earth's surface.

SUPPLIES

* I straw
* scissors
* cardboard
* tape
* electrical wire
* 3 nails
* 3 batteries
* 4 metal paper clips
* wirecutters

RAIL LAUNCHER

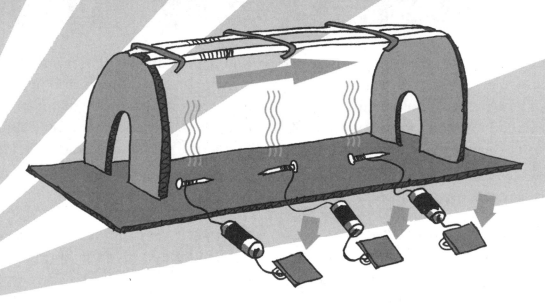

5 Place the three buttons for the three electromagnets next to each other, so that you can quickly press them one after another. Tape them in place.

6 Practice pushing your buttons in order so that as soon as the clip has been pulled to one magnet, that first one turns off, and the next one comes on. This may take some practice to get right. You should be able to get the clip to quickly zip from one end of the rail to the other, and even off the end.

The Real Thing

A full-size rail launcher would be much bigger, and would use thousands of magnets, carefully timed by computer to turn on and off. Each magnet would add a little more speed and momentum. The rail would also be curved up at the end, so that when its load is shot out the end, it would head toward space. One day such launchers may be used on the moon to send people on to Mars, or send valuable elements down to Earth.

MAKE YOUR OWN
MODEL SPACE

Another method for lifting spaceships, cargo, and people off the planet and into orbit is the space elevator. This would make it much cheaper to put things and people in space. The elevator would be made of a very long, very strong series of cables. One end would be attached to the earth, probably near the equator, in a country like Brazil or Ecuador. The other end would be attached to a large, geosynchronous satellite.

A space elevator could lift its cargo into space by using motors to climb the cable, or it could use a system of counterweights.

1 Fill the bucket with dirt or sand, Stick one end of the broomstick into the sand so it stands straight up.

2 Put one nail through the center of each spool. You are making pulleys from these. Hammer two nails into the side of the broomstick. Nail one near the top of the stick. Nail the other one into the bottom of the stick near the top of the dirt.

SUPPLIES

* bucket or large empty can
* dirt or sand
* broomstick or other long thin stick
* 2 empty thread spools
* 3 nails, slightly longer than the spools
* hammer
* 2 empty soup cans
* string

3 With the hammer and third nail, poke a hole in the center of the bottom of both cans. Poke two holes in opposite sides of the top of each can. Thread a piece of string through the two top holes and tie it off, creating a handle for the can.

4 Hook the handle of one of the cans around the nail at the top of the stick. (This is only temporary.) Thread one end of a string through the hole at the bottom of this can. Tie a knot in the end of the string coming out the top, so that it won't pass through the hole. Run the other end down the stick and wrap the other end once around the spool at the bottom. Place the second can at the bottom of the stick. Then, push the end of the string through the hole in the bottom of the second can, and tie it off with a knot as well.

ELEVATOR

5 Take another string and tie it around the handle of the bottom can. Run it up the stick and wrap it once around the top spool. Unhook the first can from the spool, and tie the end of the string to the handle of the top can.

6 Load one can with your payload—whatever you want to carry to the top of your elevator. A toy astronaut, for example, might be a good idea.

7 Load the other can at the top with enough dirt or sand to balance the weight of the load in the bottom can. When they are balanced, they should both hang at the middle of the stick. It will only take a slight push to move the elevator up or down.

90,000 MILES TALL

Some scientists are looking at building such an elevator. It might have to be over 90,000 miles tall, and could reduce the cost to put things in space to a thousandth of the current price. Since the top pulley would be a satellite in geosynchronous orbit, there would not need to be any giant broomstick like in your model. Only the strings, giant cables, would be needed.

Solar Wind Sails

O SEND A SPACECRAFT INTO ORBIT OR TO THE MOON, or to another nearby object, a rocket might be sufficient. Rockets have already taken people to the moon and back. For longer journeys though, such as to the outer planets, a rocket is impractical. Rockets burn fuel, and for a long journey, they have to carry a lot of fuel. The more fuel, the heavier the rocket. That means it requires more fuel to launch.

One solution to this problem for long-term voyages is to use solar wind sails. The solar wind isn't like the winds on Earth. Wind on Earth is caused by changes in the temperature of the air in the atmosphere. The solar wind is a stream of particles—mostly charged hydrogen and helium atoms, called **ions**—that are ejected from the sun.

Unlike the earth's wind, the solar wind doesn't change direction. It is always pushing outward from the sun. So, if you want to travel from the earth away from the sun, you can ride the solar winds. The push of the solar wind is not very strong, but a spacecraft that has a long way to go could actually build up a lot of speed from the solar wind over time. First, the spaceship would need a big sail. The sail would unfold after the space ship had been launched into space by a rocket, rail launcher, space elevator, or other means. Because the sail won't unfurl until after it is in space, it can be much bigger and much lighter in weight than it could be on Earth.

Second, the push from the solar wind will be light when the craft first starts out. But, in space, there is little to slow down the craft once it starts moving. There is no **friction** from wheels, or wind resistance. Furthermore, the solar wind will keep adding to the velocity as more particles are constantly shot out from the sun. Therefore, the speed from the first push will be added to by the second, and added to both of those by the third, etc. Eventually, a spacecraft powered by a solar wind sail could reach very high speeds.

You can build your own model of a solar-wind-powered spacecraft. Now, a real spacecraft wouldn't need the wheels, of course, and wouldn't be slowed down by the friction against the floor, or the wind resistance in the air. You will also be limited in how far you can go, but the sun will keep shining for millions of years. However, as a craft gets farther from the sun, the solar wind does get weaker, as it is spread out over a larger and larger area. Thus, it is important to build as big a sail as possible for a real spacecraft to get as much of a push as possible before getting too far away from the sun.

Solar Wind

Do not confuse the solar wind with the light that shines from the sun. The solar wind is not sunlight, but a stream of some of the particles that make up atoms. These are ejected from the sun at very high speeds. The fastest part of the solar wind leaves the sun going about two million miles per hour. That's very fast, but still slow compared to the speed of light itself, which is about 670 million miles per hour.

The solar wind doesn't travel that fast forever, though. It slows down as it travels away from the sun, because space isn't really empty. Space contains a very, very thin gas of hydrogen and helium called the interstellar medium. The solar wind slows down as it passes through that medium, so that about 94 AUs from the sun, it is only going about the speed of sound. This point is called the termination shock, and the Voyager I spacecraft passed it in 2004.

Words to Know

ion: an atom that has either fewer electons than protons, or more electrons than protons, and thus has a positive or negative electrical charge.

friction: resistance to movement.

MAKE YOUR OWN MODEL OF A SOLAR-WIND-POWERED SPACECRAFT

1 First, make wheels for your spacecraft. Take one of the plastic lids and lay it on the cardboard. Trace around it with the pencil four times, creating four circles. Cut them out and glue them inside the lids.

2 Poke four holes in the sides of the box, two on the bottom near the front and on opposite sides of the box, and two at the back, also opposite from each other. Make sure the holes are in a straight line across the box from each other, and are big enough to fit the dowels. Slide the dowels through the holes. Make sure that the dowels spin freely in the holes.

3 Cut holes in the center of the wheels, and slide them on the ends of the dowels. Glue them in place.

4 Make a hole in the top of the box big enough to fit a straw through. Stick a straw in it. Tape six other straws to the top of this straw, radiating away from the first one like a star, flower or web.

5 Tape the plastic wrap over the straws, creating a sail. Place your craft on a flat surface. Aim your fan or hair dryer at the sail, and turn it on. Watch your craft go. Run behind it with the fan or hair dryer, keeping up the push of the "solar wind."

SUPPLIES

* 4 plastic lids from yogurt cups
* cardboard
* pencil
* scissors
* glue
* 1 small cardboard box, such as a large match box or a butter box
* 2 dowels, larger than width of box
* straws
* tape
* plastic wrap
* hair dryer or fan

Ion Drive

T HE ION DRIVE IS ANOTHER FORM OF PROPULSION FOR long-range spaceflight, and it has actually been used on the European Space Agency's Smart 1 satellite and NASA's Deep Space 1 probe. To understand the ion drive, you must know what an ion is. An ion is an atom that is electrically charged. An atom is made up of a nucleus at the center and electrons in energy shells (sometimes called "orbits" though they don't really travel in orbits) around the nucleus. The nucleus is made up of protons, which have a positive electrical charge, and neutrons ("neutral ones"), which have no charge. Electrons have a negative electrical charge. If the number of electrons (and thus negative charges) around a nucleus equals the number of protons (and positive charges) within the nucleus, then the atom has a total charge of zero.

However, if the number of electrons is greater than the number of protons, the atom will be negatively charged. And, if the number of electrons is less than the number of protons, the atom will be positively charged. Any atom with a charge, either positive or negative, is called an ion.

One of the laws of physics is that like charges (positive and positive, or negative and negative) repel each other while unlike charges (positive and negative) attract each other. So, if you have two negatively charged ions next to each other, they will be pushed apart by their electrical charges. This repulsion can be used to power a spaceship, through the ion drive.

An ion drive propels a spaceship forward by pushing ions out the back of the ship. The back of the ship will have a charge. And, when similarly charged ions are placed next to the charged section, these ions will shoot out the back, also pushing the ship forward. (Remember, one of Newton's laws of motion says that for every action there is an equal and opposite reaction.) Like the solar-wind-powered sail, the initial push of the ion drive will be faint. But, as the drive continues, the speed will build up over a long time.

Use a Gravity Slingshot

Any spacecraft, whether powered by ion drives, solar sails, or other means, can benefit from the extra acceleration of a "gravity slingshot." When sending spacecraft to the far reaches of the solar system, we want to get them going as fast as possible because they have a long way to travel. The gravity slingshot works by sending a spacecraft to pass near the planet. As the craft approaches the planet, the gravity of the planet will pull the craft towards it, speeding it up. (Remember how the balls rolled down the gravity ramp sped up as they approached the bottom.) The craft must be going fast enough, and not be aimed straight at the planet, so that the craft will gain speed from passing by the planet, but not get pulled into an orbit around the planet.

For example, in March 2007, the New Horizons probe used the gravity slingshot of Jupiter to add 9,000 miles per hour to its velocity, increasing its total speed to 54,000 miles per hour. This makes it the fastest spacecraft ever launched by humans. In comparison, the Space Shuttle orbits the earth at about 17,000 miles an hour. However, even this speed is only about one-twelve-thousandth of the speed of light. Thus, it would take the probe 12,000 years to travel one light-year.

MAKE YOUR OWN
ION DRIVE SHIP

1 Cut one side off of the milk carton. Blow up the two balloons, and tie them off. Make sure that one of them can fit inside the milk carton. Place the milk carton in the pond or tub.

2 Rub the two balloons vigorously on your head. You might have a friend rub one of them with you. This builds up an electrical charge on the balloons and ionizes some atoms. You may have stuck a balloon to a wall this way.

3 Quickly place one of the charged balloons in the carton. Hold the other balloon near the back of the boat. The like charges of the two balloons should repel each other, pushing your ship along.

SUPPLIES

* empty milk carton
* scissors
* 2 balloons
* bath tub or pond

Ions

When these particles hit the magnetic field of the earth, they glow, and cause the northern and southern lights, also called the aurora borealis and the aurora australis. These are best seen near the earth's poles, because that's where the earth's magnetic field is the strongest.

DID YOU KNOW?
NASA'S DEEP SPACE 1 SPACECRAFT USED AN ION ENGINE TO FLY BY ASTEROID BRAILLE AND COMET BORRELLY.

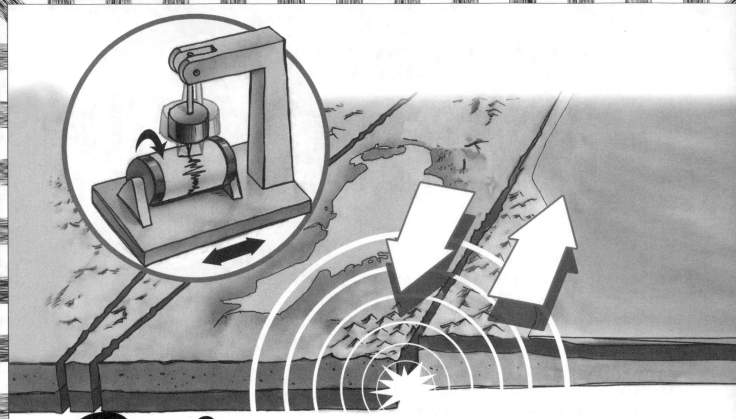

Seismometer

A SEISMOMETER IS ONE OF THE TOOLS THAT WE USE TO understand our planet, but it has also been used to learn more about other planets. The earth is seismically active, meaning that the movement of the tectonic plates over the molten mantle causes earthquakes and volcanoes. A seismometer is a tool that measures the movement of the earth. We have included seismometers on probes that have landed on other planets, such as the Viking landers on Mars.

You can make your own simple seismometer. Leave the seismometer in a secure place, where other people, pets, and wind, for example. won't disturb it. Place it as close to the ground as possible, maybe in a basement, so that sagging floors from people walking around won't move it either. Check your seismometer every day or so and see if the mark has changed. If it has, it might have been moved by a small earthquake.

Words to Know

seismic: relating to earthquakes.

MAKE YOUR OWN SIMPLE
SEISMOMETER

1 Cut notches with the craft knife in the middle of two craft sticks, halfway through the sticks and the width of the stick.

2 Slide the two sticks together to form a cross piece. This will be the base. Glue a third stick upright from the center of the base.

3 Cut some paper into strips a few inches less wide than the height of the upright stick. Wrap these strips around the upright stick, creating a roll of paper. Tape another stick at a 90-degree angle from the top of the upright stick, making an armature.

4 Tie a string to the end of the armature, hanging down in front of the roll of paper.

5 Tie the spring to the end of the string. Tie one end of another piece of string to the other end of the spring.

6 Wrap the string from the bottom of the spring around the middle of the pencil, balancing the pencil horizontally so that the tip of it is just touching the paper.

7 When you are done, place your seismometer on the floor. Jump up and down next to it, and then look at the marks on the paper. The marks on the paper have recorded the shaking to the ground your jumping caused. If you jump harder, the pencil mark will be higher. Unroll some paper to expose more unmarked paper. (A professional seismometer has a motorized spool so that there is constantly clean paper to mark, which also indicates when the seismic event takes place.) Make sure that the pencil still touches the paper. Now find that secure place and see what happens.

SUPPLIES

* craft sticks
* craft knife
* glue
* paper
* scissors
* tape
* string
* small spring from a retractable ball point pen
* small pencil

Solar-Powered Spacecraft

ONE OF THE PROBLEMS THAT MUST BE DEALT WITH IN exploring the solar system is the power source for our rovers, satellites, and spacecraft. Not only do these machines have to get where they are going, by rockets, ion drives, or other means, but they also need a power source for their cameras, sensors, computers, and communications equipment. They could carry their power with them, either stored in batteries or as fuel for generators. However, that would be very heavy, requiring more energy to be lifted into space, and they would eventually run out.

Some exploratory craft get their power from small nuclear power generators. These require fuel, but a small amount of nuclear fuel can last a very long time. Solar power is another power source used for exploring the solar system. With solar power, you don't need to carry any fuel, as the sun is constantly shooting more sunlight out into the solar system.

The Mars Rovers, for example, are powered by solar cells, which is one reason that their missions have lasted so long. They have also been fortunate that the winds on Mars periodically blow dust off of the rovers' solar collectors, keeping them clear so they can keep receiving power.

Photovoltaic cells work because they have a top layer of a semi-conductor, typically silicon with added phosphorus. The silicon forms a crystal matrix, but the extra phosphorus has one more proton and thus attracts one more electron. These extra electrons don't fit well into the matrix of silicon atoms, so they can be easily knocked loose by the photons of sunlight. These extra electrons can then power things, such as your calculator or a Mars Rover.

One day, explorers who live and work on the moon and Mars and elsewhere might supply their energy needs with solar power.

Solar Power

The first solar-powered spacecraft was the Vanguard 1, launched by the United States in 1958. It is only six inches in diameter, and while no longer operational, it is the oldest artificial satellite still in orbit around the earth.

It gets more difficult to use solar power the farther one gets from the sun, as there is less sunlight available. For example, Mars only receives half of the sunlight of Earth, and the dwarf planet Ceres only gets about 10 percent. Because of this, most solar-powered spacecraft have been designed to be used near the Earth or Mars. But recent improvements in the efficiency of solar cells means the Juno spacecraft, which is scheduled for launch in 2011, will power itself with solar energy while it orbits Jupiter.

The largest solar-powered spacecraft is the International Space Station. Each of its arrays of solar panels is over 100 feet long and almost 40 feet wide. That's quite a way to come from the six-inch-wide Vanguard 1! In the future, it may be possible for people on Earth to get their power from giant, solar-powered satellites that would collect energy and beam it down to antennas. However, we would first need to create a cheap way, like a space elevator, to get the materials to build these satellites into space.

Photovoltaic Cells

Solar cells are also called photovoltaic cells. "Photo" means light—photograph literally means writing with light—and volts are a measure of electricity. Volt was named after Alessandro Volta, the Italian physicist who invented the battery.

MAKE YOUR OWN
SOLAR-POWERED DYNAMO

* straws
* tape
* aluminum foil
* plastic soda or water bottle with cap
* water
* black plastic trash bag
* drill
* plastic tube from a ball point pen
* craft sticks
* cardboard
* metal paper clip
* small magnet
* wire

1 Build a solar reflector out of straws and aluminum foil. Make six extra-long straws by pushing the end of one straw into another. Tape six long straws together in a star pattern. Tape six other straws between the ends of the straws, making a web or net.

2 Cover the web with aluminum foil. Try to keep it as smooth as possible. This is your solar reflector.

3 Fill the plastic bottle with water. Wrap it in black plastic, and place it in the middle of the reflector. The black plastic absorbs heat.

4 Take the cap off the plastic bottle. Drill or punch a hole in the cap, slightly off-center and the size of the plastic tube. Insert the tube into the hole.

5 Drill a small hole, the diameter of a paper clip, in the end of two craft sticks. Tape the two craft sticks to either side of the cap, with the holes sticking up. They should be at a ninety degree angle to the offset hole in the cap.

6 Cut two small rectangles of cardboard, slightly less wide than the space between the two sticks and two inches long. Cut a notch halfway through in the middle of both rectangles. Slip the two rectangles together at the notches, making an "X" shape.

7 Unbend a paper clip and slide it through the two holes in the craft sticks. The clip should spin freely in the holes. Bend up one end of the clip so it will not slip out of the hole.

8 Tape the cardboard "X" to the metal paper clip so that one of the inside corners lays along the clip.

9 Wrap the other end of the paper clip around the small magnet and tape it in place. Screw the lid back on the bottle. Tape another stick or dowel to the side of the bottle, having it stick up just below the magnet.

10 Tape the middle part of a long piece of wire to the end of the stick. Coil the wire into several round coils surrounding, but not touching, the magnet. (If your wire is not stiff enough to keep the round shape, you can coil it around a section of cardboard tube, like a toilet paper tube.) The magnet should spin freely within the coils.

11 Attach the two other ends of the wire to the small light bulb. One wire should touch the base of the bulb and the other should touch the threads on the side.

12 Place the entire project in sunlight. Fold up the sides of the reflector so that the sunlight hits the plastic bottle. If you need to, prop up the sides of the reflector with rocks or blocks to keep them aimed at the bottle.

13 The sunlight will heat up the water in the bottle, creating steam. The steam will escape from the tube, spinning the cardboard fan. This will turn the magnet within the metal coils, which will generate an electrical charge in the wire, lighting the bulb. You can experiment with powering other electrical devices, such as a small radio with your solar-powered generator.

Words to Know

photovoltaic: able to produce electricity from light.

dynamo: a machine that generates electicity.

MAKE YOUR OWN
SOLAR-POWERED
COMMUNICATIONS CENTER

1 Run a wire from one of the leads on a solar cell to the threads at the lightbulb. Tape it in place.

2 Run another wire from the base of the light bulb to one end of the paper clip. Tape the paper clip down to the cardboard, and bend one end up. Tape a small piece of cardboard to the center of the paper clip so that you can push down on the clip like a button.

3 Tape a piece of wire to the cardboard underneath the paper clip, so that when you push down on the clip, it connects the circuit.

4 Tape the other end of that wire to the other lead from the solar cell.

5 Now place the device where it can get lots of sunlight. By pushing in on the button, you can turn the light on and off. You could send messages with this light in Morse code, or you could mount it on your Mars Rover model (next chapter). The actual Mars Rovers send messages to the earth in computer code by radio waves, but powered by solar cells, like yours.

SUPPLIES

* solar cells from an old calculator or watch, or home electronics kit*
* wire
* small lightbulb from a flashlight
* metal paper clip
* tape
* cardboard

*When you remove the cells from the device it should have some wires, called leads, coming from it. Make sure you don't cut those leads completely off. You'll need some of those wires to connect them to other things.

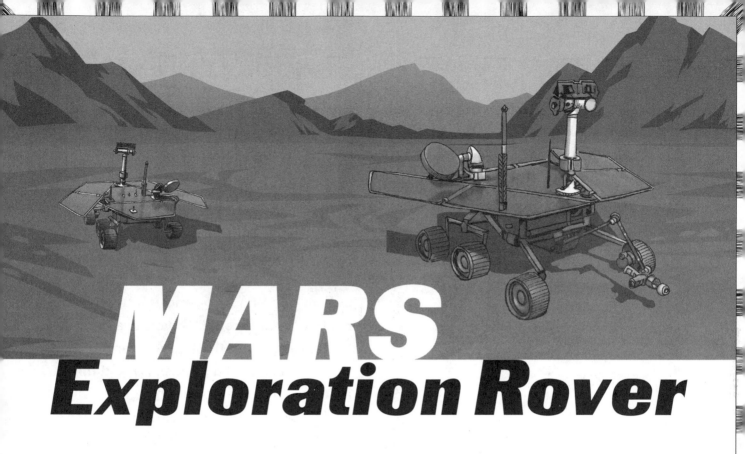

MARS
Exploration Rover

TWO OF THE GREAT SUCCESSES IN THE EXPLORATION OF THE solar system are the two Mars Exploration Rovers, named Spirit and Opportunity. They blasted off from Earth in 2003 and landed safely on Mars in 2004. These two robotic explorers were designed to last only three months on Mars, as there would be no humans around to repair them. They have so far lasted for over three years, and have gathered a huge amount of information about the Red Planet.

Each rover is equipped with scientific instruments, including cameras, magnets for gathering magnetic dust, a rock abrasion tool for scratching rocks to see beneath their surfaces, a microscope, and spectrometers. Spectrometers are tools that analyze the light (or other kinds of electromagnetic radiation, such as gamma rays, x-rays, and infra-red radiation) given off by material to identify what elements and compounds it is made of. They also are equipped with communication equipment that allows controllers on Earth to steer them, and to upload new computer programs to their on-board computers.

The Mars Exploration Rovers have used these tools to discover much about Mars, including gathering evidence that Mars may have had liquid water on it at some time in the past. This is important because it means it is possible that there was life on Mars at some point in the past.

MAKE YOUR OWN
MARS EXPLORATION

SUPPLIES

* 6 plastic soda bottle caps
* drill
* large toothpicks or wooden skewers for dowels
* craft knife
* 6 rubber bands
* paper clip
* scissors
* duct tape
* glue
* popsicle sticks
* small cardboard box such as a kitchen matches box
* lip balm tube
* cardboard
* black construction paper
* pencil
* toilet paper tubes
* paint
* markers

1 Drill a hole in the center of each lid the size of your dowels. Use the craft knife to cut a slit in the side of each cap, big enough to push a rubber band through. If you are having difficulty getting the rubber band through, unbend a paper clip and make a hook. Push the hook through the slit and hook the rubber band around the paper clip, and then pull the clip and rubber band through the slit. Wrap the rubber band around the outside of the cap, and let the remainder of the band hang on the inside of the cap.

2 Cut a one inch-piece of toothpick or skewer to make a dowel. Attach the other end of the rubber band to the middle of the dowel. Tape the band in place with duct tape and then glue it. It is important that the dowel not spin within the rubber band. Slip one end of the dowel into the hole in the cap. Don't glue this end in place. This end should rotate freely. Do this for all six caps.

ROVERS

3 Cut two popsicle sticks in half, making four half sticks. Drill a small hole the size of the dowels in the ends of the four half sticks, and two other, full-length sticks. Slide the other end of the dowels into the hole in the popsicle stick and glue in place. Glue four of the popsicle sticks to the sides of the match box.

4 Attach two other dowels to the ends of the remaining two sticks angled like the armatures that support the front two wheels of the rover.

5 Make another armature of two sticks and tape it to the right front side. This models the arm that each rover has, with sensors and a camera mounted on it. This allows the rovers to look at objects on Mars close up. Mount a small tube, like a lip balm tube, on the arm for the camera.

6 Cut out a sheet of cardboard and a piece of black construction paper to match Template F at the back of the book. Glue the construction paper on to the cardboard, and glue both to the top of the box. These represent the solar cells that power the rovers. Use a ruler to draw straight lines on the construction paper representing the gridwork of solar cells.

Naming the Rovers

The two rovers were named in an essay contest of school children. The winning essay was written by Sofi Collis, a nine-year-old girl from Arizona, who was born in Russia. Her essay says:

"I used to live in an Orphanage.

It was dark and cold and lonely.

At night, I looked up at the sparkly sky and felt better.

I dreamed I could fly there.

In America, I can make all my dreams come true . . .

7 Cut a toilet paper tube lengthwise on only one side, and then roll it back over itself until it is about half of its normal thickness and tape it back together. Do this a second time with another tube. Pierce a hole the size of a pencil through the middle of one tube, sideways, and then run a pencil through that hole, and then through the middle, lengthwise of the second tube. Tape the two tubes together, forming a "T" shape. This represents the mast of the rover, which has cameras and other sensors mounted on it. Mount your mast on the front of the rover by piercing another hole in the cardboard, as marked on the template. Tape or glue the mast in place.

8 Make another skinny toilet paper tube like those you made above. Cut two pieces of cardboard to match Template G. Cut out another piece of cardboard to match Template H. Glue the three pieces together to form a thick paddle, and then glue them to the tube. Attach all of this to the top of the rover. This represents the radio transmitter and receiver that allows the rover to communicate with Earth and send back pictures and other information about Mars. Now your model is complete. If you hold it firmly and pull backward on a flat surface, you will wind up the rubber bands inside the wheel assemblies. Release the rover and it will roll forward on its own.

9 If you like, you can decorate your model with paint and markers. Write "NASA" and "Spirit" or "Opportunity" on it, or give it your own name. You can also mount your solar-powered light from the previous activity on top of your rover.

DID YOU KNOW?

THE FIRST SUCCESSFUL MARS ROVER, THE MARS PATHFINDER, WHICH LANDED ON MARS IN 1997, WAS NAMED SOJOURNER. IT WAS NAMED FOR THE AFRICAN AMERICAN ABOLITIONIST, SOJOURNER TRUTH.

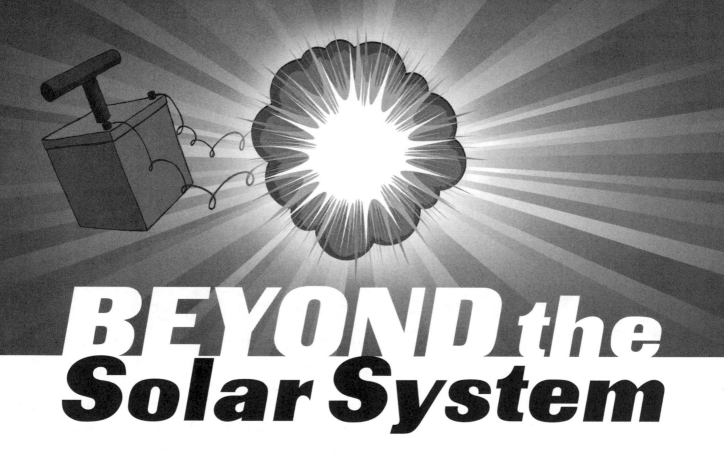

BEYOND the Solar System

S O NOW WE KNOW WHAT IS IN THE SOLAR SYSTEM, AND HOW we learned about it. But, how was the solar system created? Where did it come from? How old is it? To understand the history of the solar system, we must first go back to the history of the universe itself.

About 14 billion years ago, the entire universe was concentrated into an infinitely small, dense, hot mass of energy. It exploded, expanding and cooling in an event called the "Big Bang."

In the early moments of the expansion, this energy cooled down into **electrons**, **protons**, and **neutrons**, (and other sub-atomic particles,) the basic units of matter. These still had so much energy for the first million years (or so) of the universe that the protons and electrons couldn't connect with each other to form atoms. At this point, all of the matter in the universe was still in the form of a plasma, which is like a gas, but made of **ionized nuclei** and free electrons. Ionized nuclei are ones that have a charge. In this case, it is because they have no electrons, which have a negative charge, to balance the positive charge of the protons in the **nucleus**.

Eventually the universe expanded and cooled down enough to allow the **electromagnetic** attraction between electrons and protons to form atoms. In these early millions of years of the universe, only the lightest and simplest elements were created—hydrogen, helium, and a small amount of lithium. These have only one, two, and three protons in their nuclei, respectively.

Words to Know

electron: a small particle that makes up atoms, has a negative charge, and exists outside the nucleus.

proton: a heavy particle that makes up atoms, is in the nucleus, and has a positive charge.

neutron: a heavy particle that makes up atoms, is in the nucleus, and has no charge.

nucleus: the center of an atom, made up of protons and neutrons. The plural is nuclei.

ionized nuclei: nucleus with a charge.

electromagnetic: one of the fundamental forces of the universe, which is responsible for magnetic attraction and electrical charges.

nebulae: giant interstellar clouds of gas and dust. The singular is nebula.

supernova: the explosion of a giant star.

The Birth of Stars

Once atoms cooled, these elements were scattered across the still expanding universe. They were not spread out evenly, however, but were clustered into irregular clumps. The gravity between these atoms pulled them toward each other. Over millions of years, these formed into larger and larger clouds of gas, called **nebulae.**

Beautiful Nebulae

Nebulae can appear quite beautiful, with many colors caused by varying amounts of different gases. People also see shapes of other objects in the shapes of the nebulae, just as you may see shapes in the water vapor clouds on Earth. For example, two famous nebulae are called the Horse Head Nebula and the Eagle Nebula.

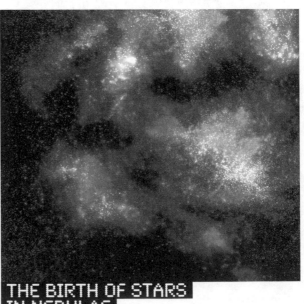

THE BIRTH OF STARS IN NEBULAE

These nebulae eventually concentrated their matter into such large central balls of gas that the heat and pressure in the center of these balls fused the hydrogen in their centers into helium. This nuclear fusion creates light and heat, creating a star. These first stars, called first-generation stars, had no Earth-like planets around them. This is because for the first several millions of years of the universe, there was no iron, silicon, or any of the other elements that make up the terrestrial planets.

Even though stars are not alive in the way we say plants or animals are alive, stars do have a lifespan. Stars are "born" in nebulae, clouds of interstellar gas and dust, when enough gas, mostly hydrogen, is pulled together by gravity to undergo nuclear fusion. Stars fuse their hydrogen for millions and billions of years and then they "die," which means that they stop fusing hydrogen in different ways depending on the size of the star.

The life and existence of a star depends upon a balancing act or tug of war btween two competing forces. The force of the gravity of the star, whose strength depends upon the total mass of the star, attempts to collapse or squeeze the star into a very small and dense clump of matter. The energetic fusion reaction of the star, which creates the light and heat of the sun that we see and feel, also pushes the star outward, fighting against gravitational collapse. As long as the supply of hydrogen fuel for that fusion reaction lasts, the star will remain stable. Once it begins to run out, however, it will go through changes. The types of changes depend upon the size of the star.

Supernovas

Stars that are much bigger than the sun, about ten times as big or more, go through

SUPERNOVA

Galaxies

Most stars in the universe are gathered into large clusters called galaxies. Our solar system is in the Milky Way Galaxy, which includes hundreds of billions of stars. Most of those stars are collected in the center of the galaxy, known as the nucleus or core. The galaxy is mostly a flat disk of stars, about 120,000 light-years across, but it bulges at the core. Spreading out from the nucleus are arms that spiral outward. The Milky Way has five of these: the Cygnus, Perseus, Orion, Sagittarius, and Norma arms. The sun, and thus the solar system, including the earth, is located in the Orion Arm, about 30,000 light-years from the galactic nucleus, or center.

many changes. Once these bigger stars reach the point at which their helium fusion has stopped, their gravity will be so large, and create so much pressure, that its carbon core will fuse into other elements, such as silicon, magnesium, and oxygen. Eventually, some of these elements will be fused into iron. At this point the iron will get so heavy and dense that it will collapse in on itself. Then, the iron will be converted into neutrons, which will slam into each other so hard tht they will bounce back outwards. This bounce will slam into the last bits of hot, glowing gas that surrounded the star, blowing that gas outwards with amazing force. This colossal explosion is called a **supernova**. Nova means "new." Supernovas are so bright that to the naked eye it can appear that a new star has been created, when in fact an old star has just exploded. It looks like a new star has appeared because the old one was too faint to be seen before it exploded.

The energy and heat during the explosion of a supernova are so incredibly powerful that it creates heavier elements. Every element heavier than iron, such as gold, silver, lead, tin, and uranium is formed in these explosions.

After a few hundreds of millions of years, some of the very largest of these first-generation stars burned up most of their hydrogen and went through the process described above. When these first supernovae exploded, they scattered the elements they created throughout the galaxy. The remnants from many of these supernovae flew through space until they encountered

other remnants of other supernovae. These were eventually slowed down and pulled together by gravity and collected into new nebulae.

These new clouds of dust and gas were very similar to those out of which the first stars formed, but they had one important difference. While still mostly made of hydrogen and helium, they also had small amounts of all of the other naturally occurring elements. Therefore, it was now possible for terrestrial planets made of iron and silicon and other elements to form from these second-generation nebulae.

The Birth of Planets

These new nebulae went through the same process of being pulled together by gravity until the center of the cloud gathered enough mass to become a star. At the same time, the gravitational pull caused

DID YOU KNOW?

THE BRIGHT BAND OF STARS THAT WE SEE IN THE SKY AND CALL THE MILKY WAY IS THE SAGITTARIUS ARM AND GALACTIC CENTER OF THE MILKY WAY GALAXY. OTHER CULTURES HAVE NAMED THIS BRIGHT BAND THE BIRD'S PATH (TURKISH), THE SILVERY RIVER (CHINESE), THE STRAW WAY (AFRICA), AND THE WAY THE DOG RAN AWAY (CHEROKEE.)

You Are Made From the Stars

One of the amazing things about the history of the solar system is that the nebula from which it formed could only have come about after first-generation stars were born, burned out, and then exploded as supernovae, many light-years away. All of the elements heavier than lithium on the earth (including the iron that makes up much of the earth and the oxygen you breathe) were created in supernovae. You take in these elements when you eat, drink, and breathe and turn them into the cells of your body.

Thus, you and everyone you know are made from the products of the nuclear furnaces of stars that exploded billions of years ago. You are, literally, made from the stars.

the cloud to begin to spin. Imagine you and a friend facing each other with your arms stretched towards each other with your palms touching. If you were to push against each other without letting up, eventually you would fall to one side or the other. The same thing happens with the nebula, but since the gravity keeps pulling the cloud together, it continues to spin in one direction. This spinning causes the nebulae to flatten out, turning it into a mostly flat disk. This is the beginning of a solar system.

At various points along this disk, other concentrations of matter began to form planets. About four and a half billion years ago, in one such second-generation nebula in the Orion Arm of the Milky Way Galaxy, a concentration of iron and other elements began to form about 93 million miles from the center of our solar system. This was the beginnings of the earth. At other spots throughout the nebula, other bits of dust and gas were pulled together, forming other planets and asteroids.

However, the earth's creation wasn't a calm process. These bits of iron and silicon dust were pulled together by gravity, forming larger and larger concentrations of elements. These were still spinning around the center of the cloud at high speeds. So the solar system had a large number of flying, spinning rocks. These rocks collided with each other, sometimes shattering, sometimes bouncing off each other, and sometimes hitting with such force that they melted and fused together, forming bigger rocks. Larger and larger rocks formed, which gave them greater concentrations of gravity, causing them to pull each other together with even more force. The surface of the earth was probably covered with an ocean of magma at this time because of the energy from all

these impacts. This period lasted for millions of years and was called the Great Bombardment. These collisions added both mass and energy to the newly formed planet. The earth still has a molten core in part because of the leftover heat and energy from that time.

This description of the formation of the solar system is called the Nebular Hypothesis, and it explains a lot of the characteristics of our system. For one, most of the planets orbit the sun along the plane of the flattened disk that was formed by the spinning of the nebula. Two, most orbit the sun in the same direction, and mostly rotate in that direction as well, which is the same direction that the sun itself rotates on its axis. Almost all the moons

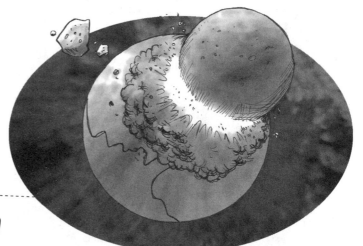

Earth's Moon

There is another very important remnant from the time of the Great Bombardment—Luna, our moon. About 35 million years after the earth first formed, another planet called Theia smashed into the earth. It hit at just the right angle to throw a huge amount of the mantle of the earth into orbit around the earth. This material from Earth's mantle, as well as the leftovers of Theia, were pulled together through accretion to form the moon. This explanation for the creation of the moon is sometimes called the "Big Splash."

that orbit the planets do so in this same direction. Some of the gas giants' moons orbit it in the opposite direction, which suggests that those moons did not form around their planets, but may have formed elsewhere in the solar system and were later trapped by the giants' incredible gravitational pull as they flew by.

The Future of Our Solar System

You don't have to worry about our sun becoming a supernova. Our sun is not big enough for that to happen. Our sun does have a lifespan and will "burn out," but in a less spectacular way. Stars about the size of our sun go through a period of turning hydrogen into helium until most of the hydrogen in the core is used up. Once that happens, the force of gravity will overcome the weakened outward push of fusion and the star will shrink. This will increase the pressure and heat in the center of the star, causing the helium that is created by hydrogen fusion to fuse into carbon. During this process, the star will expand, getting larger,

and the surface will become cooler. When this happens our sun will become a type of star called a red giant, and will enlarge so much that it will swallow up Mercury. It will actually expand beyond the present day orbit of Venus, but it will push Venus into a farther orbit, so only Mercury will be within the diameter of the red giant stage. You still don't need to worry because this won't happen for a few billion years.

After the red giant period, the sun (and other stars about its size) will run out of helium to fuse into carbon. It will then collapse into a very small, but very dense, ball of carbon about the volume of the earth, but many times more massive. Its surface will be quite hot, and will continue giving off light and heat as it cools down, even though it will no longer be fusing one element into another. This kind of star is called a white dwarf.

After many more millions of years, it will eventually cool down completely. The planets will continue to orbit the cold sun in darkness. This will be the final bow of our solar system, though not of our galaxy or the universe. It won't be until billions and billions of years in the future. By then, our decendants may have spread to other star systems circling younger stars, carrying with them the life that was created in our solar system.

BIG BANG Balloon

THE ASTRONOMER EDWIN HUBBLE DISCOVERED MANY things about the universe. One of the strangest things he discovered was that galaxies are moving away from our galaxy, and from each other. Not only that, but the farther away from each other they are, the faster the galaxies are moving away from each other. The explanation that best makes sense of these observations is that the universe itself is expanding.

Imagine that you and your friends are running away from each other in a gymnasium, and that you represent the galaxies. Now imagine that you are not only running as fast as you can, but that the gym itself is expanding as you run. If the gym floor expands at a rate of 10 percent per second, for example, then your friends who are farthest away from you will be moving away from you the fastest. For example, there is 10 feet between you and your friend Bill, and 100 feet between you and your friend Sally. After one second, Bill will be 11 feet from you, or one foot farther, and Sally will be 110 feet away, or 10 feet further.

If the universe is expanding, then it is possible to imagine this process in reverse, like rewinding a film. By doing the mathematical calculations to rewind this expansion, they developed the concept of the Big Bang. This is the concept that the universe expanded from a nearly infinitely small and nearly infinitely dense single point, and then exploded at a moment about 14 billion years ago into the expanding universe we live in now.

MAKE YOUR OWN
BIG BANG BALLOON

1 Lay the balloon on a flat surface. Draw a number of galaxies on the balloon by placing many tiny dots, representing stars on the surface of the balloon. Make your clusters of dots into the shapes of galaxies. Many galaxies are either elliptical or spiral in shape. Flip the balloon over and do the same on the other side. Let the ink from your marker dry.

2 Blow up your balloon. Stop frequently while blowing up the balloon to check the progress. Watch as the galaxies move further from each other as the universe expands.

SUPPLIES

* un-inflated balloon, black if you can get it
* thin tipped marker (silver, gold, white or yellow would be good, but the marker and balloon must be different colors)

What is a Nebula?

A NEBULA IS A GIANT CLOUD OF GAS IN OUTER SPACE. NEBulae (the plural of nebula) are sometimes called "stellar nurseries" because that is where stars are "born." A nebula may stretch for millions of miles and contains huge amounts of gases. The majority of this gas is hydrogen, the most common element in the universe. But, a nebula also includes smaller amounts of nearly every element in the universe.

All the gas atoms, like all matter, are attracted to other atoms by gravity. As two atoms are attracted to each other, their collective, greater mass will have a greater gravitational pull on nearby atoms. By pulling more atoms into larger and larger groups, those groups will have greater gravitational pull, pulling in more atoms, creating even greater concentrations of mass, which have greater gravitational pull, pulling in more atoms, etc. This type of ongoing process that gets stronger as it goes is sometimes called a positive feedback loop.

Over many thousands of years, some of the gas of a nebula, which is spread out over a very large area, becomes concentrated in a small area. That ball of gas pulls itself inward because of its great mass and gravity. This can eventually create a great amount of heat and pressure in the center of this gas. If the pressure and heat are high enough because the ball of gas is massive enough, the hydrogen will fuse into helium. This process, called fusion, gives off heat and energy. When a gas ball ignites in this way, it becomes a star.

MAKE YOUR OWN
BEAUTIFUL NEBULA PICTURE

1 Lay newspaper on your work surface under the cooling rack. Food coloring can stain your clothes, so be careful. You might want to wear old clothes.

2 Trim several sheets of paper so that they will fit flat in the dish without bending. Remove them from the dish. Pour enough water into the dish to just cover the bottom with an even layer.

3 Add a few drops of different colors of food coloring to the water. Add them carefully and let them mingle gently. You might gently intermingle them with your fork, but don't stir them vigorously. You don't want them to mix. Try to get the clouds of color to look like pictures of nebulae. You can look on the Internet for pictures. Experiment, and if it gets all mixed up, just pour it out and try again.

4 Gently lay the paper down on the surface of the water. Don't submerge it completely. Again, experiment with what works best. Remove the paper carefully and lay it, colored side up, on the cooling rack

to dry. Your paper should now have colored cloud patterns like a nebula. Experiment as many times as you want until you get some nebula shapes that you like.

5 Once the paper has dried, glue some glitter on the paper for the stars that are born in your nebula. Don't overdo it.

6 Look at the shapes that formed in your nebula, and give it a name. Nebulae often have beautiful, descriptive names. Now you can hang it on your wall, put it in your notebook, or use it for decoration.

SUPPLIES

- ★ cooling rack
- ★ newspaper
- ★ wide, shallow baking dish, like a casserole dish
- ★ paper
- ★ scissors
- ★ water
- ★ food coloring
- ★ fork
- ★ glitter and glue

Pulsar Model

THE UNIVERSE CONTAINS MANY INTERESTING THINGS BEsides just stars and planets like our own. One of the weirdest and most unusual of these things is called a pulsar, meaning a thing that pulses.

A **pulsar** is a kind of **neutron star**. A neutron star is what is left over after a supernova. All of the iron that was formed in the core of the giant star before the supernova exploded is crushed together until all of its protons and electrons change into neutrons. This makes a very dense star, made up of neutrons. The neutron star will eject electromagnetic energy, such as radio waves, out its north and south magnetic poles. At the same time, the neutron star rotates on its axis. Like the earth, the rotational axis, and the magnetic poles are not at the exact same place on the star. This means that as the pulsar rotates, the stream of electromagnetic energy sweeps across the sky, shining on one part of the sky before moving on.

When the pulsar shines on the earth, and then rotates away, and then rotates all the way around to shine on the earth again, it appears as if it is turning on and off, when it is really just spinning. You can demonstrate this property.

Words to Know

pulsar: a neutron star that rotates and emits energy, appearing to pulse as it rotates.

neutron star: a star that has collapsed under its gravity and whose atoms have all converted to neutrons.

MAKE YOUR OWN
PULSAR MODEL

SUPPLIES

* pencil
* CD
* ball of clay
* small flashlight
* tape
* dark room

1 Place the pencil through the center of the CD. Use the clay to hold the pencil in place. You are making a device like a top.

2 Tape the flashlight across the CD, perpendicular to the pencil. Most pulsars will have their magnetic poles and rotational axis closer together than this, but this will still give you an idea of what is going on.

3 Turn on the flashlight, and turn off the lights in your dark room. Spin the top on the floor or a table or counter. Focus your sight at the flashlight as it shines at you. When the light is pointed directly at you, it appears to blink on and off, like a pulsar. Because you are in a room you will see the light also bouncing off the walls. But

Pulsars

Pulsars were first discovered in 1967 and were briefly, and perhaps not very seriously, thought to be some sort of interstellar beacon, such as a lighthouse. These pulsars seemed to send out a strong pulse of electromagnetic energy. Because the pulsars seemed to blink regularly, like someone turning a light switch on and off, some thought that they might have been artificially created, which would suggest the existence of extraterrestrial (meaning off of the earth) intelligent life. Unfortunately for the search for extraterrestrial intelligence, pulsars are naturally occurring objects in space. However, they are fascinating on their own and worth studying.

in outer space, there is very little for the beam to bounce off, so it looks like the pulsar is only winking at you. Try it ouside at night to see the difference.

DID YOU KNOW?

THE EARTH SENDS OUT PULSES OF ITS OWN THAT, UNLIKE A PULSAR, ARE SIGNS OF INTELLIGENT LIFE. ALL OF OUR RADIO AN TELEVISION BROADCASTS LEAVE THE EARTH AT THE SPEED OF LIGHT, AND COULD BE PICKED UP BY AN ALIEN CIVILIZATION.

LIGHT-YEARS
and Parsecs

HEN WE LOOK AT THINGS WITHIN THE SOLAR SYSTEM we can use the AU, the astronomical unit, for comparing distances. The earth is one AU from the sun, Pluto is about 40, etc. So how big is the whole solar system? There is not a hard and fast border or boundary on the edge of the solar system, but we generally believe that the edge of the Oort Cloud is about 200 AU from the sun.

That makes the solar system about 400 AU across, from one side of the Oort Cloud, past the sun and to the other side of the cloud. That's really big. But, when we get outside the solar system, we have to use even bigger units of measurement. The main unit of measurement outside the solar system is the **light-year**. The light-year is the distance that light travels in a year, which is 186,000 miles per second. This is almost 670 million miles an hour. It only takes light about eight minutes to travel the 93 million miles (1 AU) from the sun to the earth.

In a whole year, light travels almost 6 trillion miles. This is more than 63,000 AU. You would have to travel more than a light-year to get to the nearest star. In fact, the nearest star, Proxima Centauri, is about 4.2 light-years away. On average, stars in our galaxy are 3.3 light-years apart from each other. Coincidentally, this is also about the same as a unit called the **Parsec**. "Parsec" is short for Parallax of one Second of arc. In this case, a second is not a unit of time, but a measurement of angle.

MAKE YOUR OWN SOLAR SYSTEM MODEL

You can make a scale model of the width of the solar system and a light-year. If you still have your AU model set up, you can put this one next to it.

1 Paint the pea yellow. This represents the sun. Let it dry, and glue it to the top of a toothpick.

2 Cut out 13 small triangles of construction paper, and glue each triangle to a toothpick, making small flags.

3 Label one flag for each of the four terrestrial planets: Mercury, Venus, Mars, Earth. Label one for each of the Jovian planets: Jupiter, Saturn, Uranus and Neptune. Then label two for the Kuiper Belt, and one each for the dwarf planets of Ceres, Pluto, Eris, and Sedna.

4 Place your sun pea at the goal line of one end of the field. Place your other flags at a scale distance from the sun. For this model, we are using the scale of one foot for one AU. So use your ruler to measure one AU from the sun and place the earth flag there. Remember your AU model on the larger scale, with the earth as a pea and the sun as a two-foot ball. On this scale, the distance of that whole model fits within this one foot measure, and the two-foot sun is only a pea. The planets have to be represented by flags because planet models to scale would be too small to see.

5 Place the Mercury flag four inches from the sun. Place the Venus flag about nine inches from the sun. Place the Mars flag six inches past the earth flag.

How Far is Far?

To think about the mind-boggling distances of space, first imagine 4.2 light-years. That is the distance to the nearest star from the sun. Next, try to imagine 120,000 light-years. That is the distance across our galaxy, the Milky Way. Finally, imagine 2 million light-years. That is the distance to the nearest galaxy, the Andromeda Galaxy.

DID YOU KNOW?

EVEN TRAVELING AS FAST AS THE FASTEST CURRENT SPACESHIP, AT FIFTY THOUSAND MILES AN HOUR, IT WOULD TAKE OVER 50,000 YEARS TO REACH THE NEAREST STAR, PROXIMA CENTAURI.

6 Place the Jovian planets next. Remember that each foot represents one AU. If you are doing this on a football field, remember that the field is marked out in yards, so each yard represents 3 AU. Place Jupiter at five feet. Place Saturn at nine and a half feet. Place Uranus at 19 feet. Place Neptune at 30-feet.

7 Now you are going to mark the boundaries of the Kuiper Belt. Place one Kuiper Belt flag at the 30-foot (10-yard) line, and place the other one 100 AU from the sun, at 100 feet.

8 Now you can mark the minor or dwarf planets. Pluto on average is about 39 AU from the sun, but its orbit is elliptical, so sometimes it is actually closer to the sun than Neptune. Eris should be placed at 97 AU. Ceres lives in the Asteroid Belt between Mars and Jupiter at 3 AU. Sedna is the farthest object out in the Kuiper Belt.

SUPPLIES

- ⋆ pea
- ⋆ yellow paint
- ⋆ glue
- ⋆ toothpicks
- ⋆ construction paper
- ⋆ scissors
- ⋆ pen or markers
- ⋆ soccer or football field, or other large field
- ⋆ ruler
- ⋆ measuring tape

Words to Know

light-year: a unit of distance defined as the distance light travels in a year, about 6 trillion miles.

Parsec: a unit of distance equal to 3.258 light-years.

The Outer Boundary

The solar system may be even larger than this, in that the Oort Cloud may stretch as far out as 50,000 AU from the sun. At the scale of your model, that would be almost 10 miles away.

MAKE YOUR OWN
MODEL OF A LIGHT-YEAR

Now, we are going to make a model of a light-year next to our model of the solar system. The distance from the sun to the edge of the Kuiper Belt is about 100 AU. That will become our new basic unit of measurement for our model of the light-year. To (almost) fit into our field, we are going to make our basic unit, of 100 AU, equal to six inches.

1 Cut out 4 triangles of construction paper. Glue the triangles to the sticks, making four flags. Label the flags: Sun, Edge of the Kuiper Belt, Edge of the Oort Cloud, One Light-year.

2 Place the flag marked "Sun" at one end of the field. Place the flag for the Edge of the Kuiper Belt six inches from the sun. Thus, at this scale, the other model of the solar system all fits within six inches.

3 Place the flag marked Edge of the Oort Cloud at the 83-yard line. This represents about 50,000 AU. Place the flag marked One Light-year about five yards into the end zone opposite the sun.

4 Now stand next to your sun flags and look across your models. All the distance in the first model, of 1 AU, fits within the first foot of the solar system model. All of the distance of the second model fits within the first six inches of the third model of the light-year.

To think about the mind-boggling distances of space, first imagine 4.2 light-years. That is the distance to the nearest star to the sun. Next, try to imagine 120,000 light-years. That is the distance across our galaxy, the Milky Way. Finally, imagine two million light-years. That is the distance to the nearest galaxy, the Andromeda Galaxy.

SUPPLIES

* construction paper
* scissors
* 4 sticks
* glue
* marker

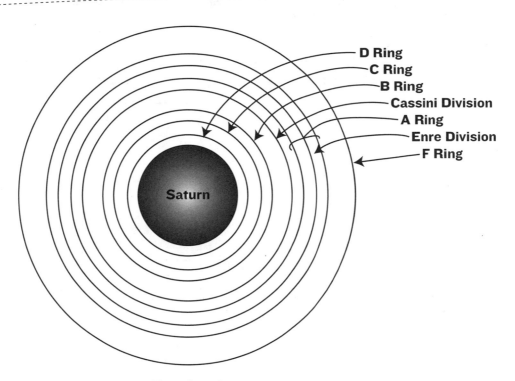

- D Ring
- C Ring
- B Ring
- Cassini Division
- A Ring
- Enre Division
- F Ring

Saturn

Template A

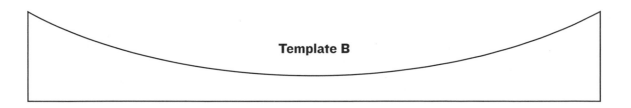

Template B

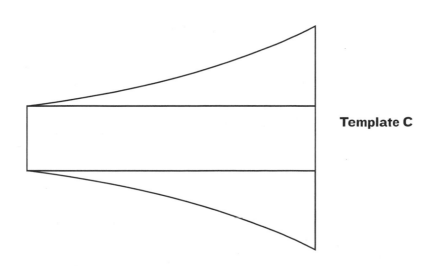

Template C

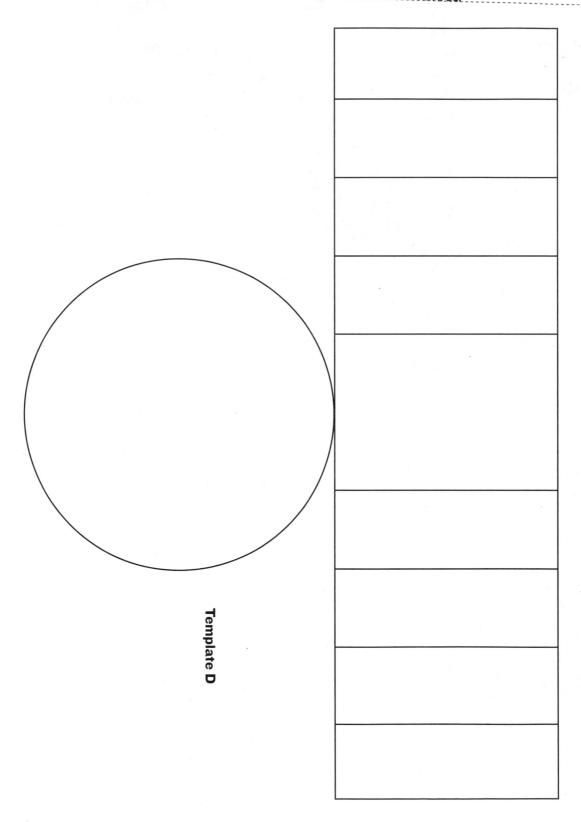

Template D

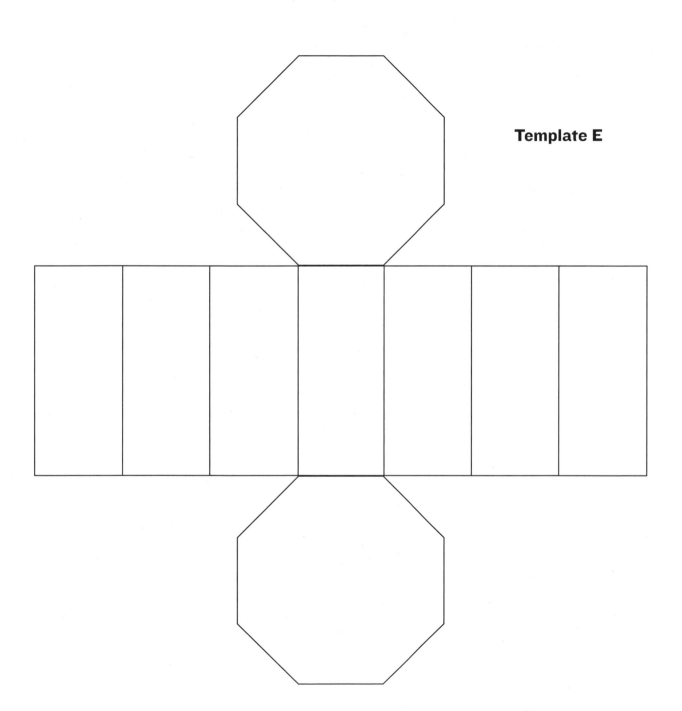

Template E

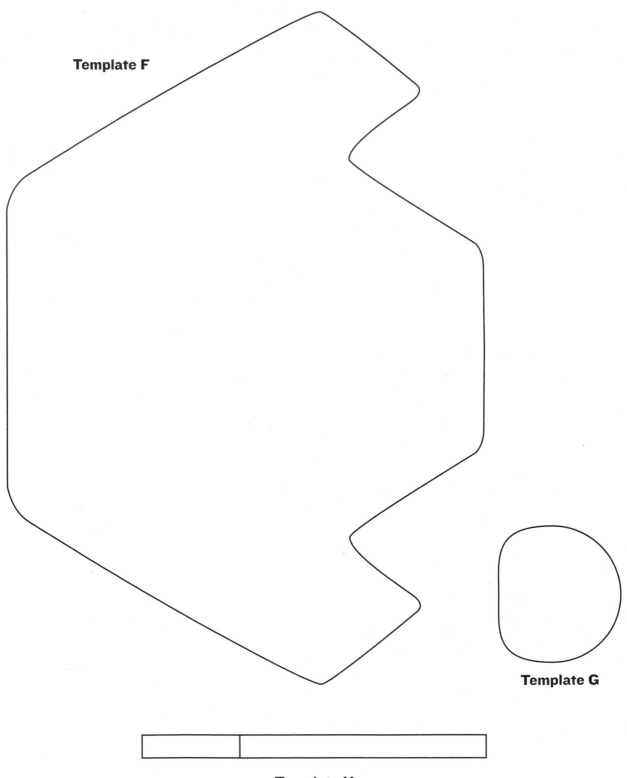

Template F

Template G

Template H

Glossary

acceleration: the process of increasing the speed of an object's movement.

accretion: the process by which larger bodies are created from the attraction of smaller bodies.

asteroids: rocky objects that orbit the sun and that are smaller than the major planets.

Astronomical Unit: a unit of distance defined by the average distance between the earth and the sun, about 93 million miles.

atmosphere: the air or gas surrounding a planet.

atom: the smallest particle of matter.

axis of rotation: an imaginary line through a planet's poles, around which it rotates.

celestial bodies: planets, moons, asteroids, comets, stars, and galaxies.

Ceres: asteroid and dwarf planet, the first and largest asteroid discovered.

comets: balls of ice and dust that orbit the sun.

convection: the transfer of heat from one region to another by the movement of a gas or liquid.

crater: round pit in the moon or other celestial body caused by the impact of a meteorite.

dynamo: a machine that generates electricity.

Einstein: Albert Einstein (1879–1955), a German/Swiss/American physicist who created the theory of relativity.

electron: a small particle that makes up atoms, has a negative charge, and exists outside the nucleus.

electromagnetic: one of the fundamental forces of the universe, which is responsible for magnetic attraction and electrical charges.

element: a pure substance that cannot be broken down into a simpler substance, and contains only one type of atom.

elliptical: shaped like an ellipse, or an oval.

friction: resistance to movement.

fusion reaction: produces the energy output of the sun when hydrogen nuclei react to form helium.

galaxy: a collection of star systems.

geocentrism: the belief, now disproved, that the earth is the center of the solar system.

geosynchronous: orbiting the earth at the same speed at which the earth rotates, so that the object remains in place over the same spot on the earth's surface.

gravity: the force that pulls all objects with mass towards each other.

gravity well: the distortion in the fabric of space-time created by the mass of an object, and into which other objects fall.

heliocentrism: the belief that the sun is the center of the solar system.

helium: the next most common element in the universe after hydrogen.

hydrogen: the most common element in the universe, and one of the elements of water.

ion: an atom that has either fewer electrons than protons, or more electrons than protons, and thus has a positive or negative electrical charge.

ionized nuclei: nucleus with a charge.

iron: an element that is a common metal.

Jovian planets: Jupiter, Saturn, Uranus, and Neptune.

Kuiper Belt: comets and asteroids that orbit the sun in a large belt at about 100 AU.

KBOs: Kuiper Belt Objects—planetoids and dwarf planets that exist in the Kuiper Belt, including Pluto and Eris.

light-year: a unit of distance defined as the distance light travels in a year, about 6 trillion miles.

mare: dark area on the moon of solidified lava. From the Latin for "sea," the plural is maria.

meteor: the streak of light when a small bit of rock or ice, from an asteroid or comet, enters the earth's atmosphere.

meteoroid: a meteor revolving around the sun.

Milky Way Galaxy: the galaxy in which the solar system is located.

momentum: the force that a moving object has in the direction that it is moving.

moon: a celestial body orbiting a larger planet.

nebulae: giant interstellar clouds of gas and dust, the singular is nebula.

neutron: a heavy particle that makes up atoms, is in the nucleus, and has no charge.

neutron star: a star that has collapsed under its gravity and whose atoms have all converted to neutrons.

Newton: Sir Isaac Newton (1643–1727), an English mathematician and physicist who discovered laws of motion and gravity.

nuclear: relating to the nucleus of an atom.

nucleus: the center of an atom, made up of protons and neutrons. The plural is nuclei.

Oort Cloud: hypothetical spherical cloud of comets at the edge of the solar system, 50,000 AU.

orbit: the path in space an object makes as it revolves around another object.

parallax: the apparent change in position of a star compared to the stars behind it, as viewed from one side of the earth's orbit around the sun and compared to the view from the other side, half a year later.

Parsec: a unit of distance equal to 3.258 light-years.

Phaeton: hypothetical historical planet that was ripped apart creating the asteroid belt.

photovoltaic: able to produce electricity from light.

planet: one of the large celestial bodies that orbit around the sun.

planetesimal: small bits of matter that come together to form planets.

planetoid: a small celestial body resembling a planet.

proton: a heavy particle that makes up atoms, is in the nucleus, and has a positive charge.

pulsar: a neutron star that rotates and emits energy, appearing to pulse as it rotates.

radiation: the process by which energy like light or sound moves from its source and radiates outward.

satellite: an object that orbits a larger object in space, whether natural or artificial.

seismic: relating to earthquakes.

solar system: the sun with the celestial bodies that orbit it.

solar wind: the stream of electrically charged particles emitted by the sun.

spectrometer: a device used to identify chemical composition by analyzing light waves.

sublimation: to change from a solid to a gas, or from a gas to a solid, without being a liquid in between.

supernova: the explosion of a giant star.

tectonic plates: large sections of the earth's crust, that move on top of the layer, the mantle, beneath.

terrestrial planets: Mercury, Venus, Earth, and Mars.

TNOs: Trans-Neptunian Objects, such as comets, planetoids, and dwarf planets that exist beyond the orbit of Neptune, including the Kuiper Belt and Oort Cloud.

universe: everything that exists everywhere.

volcanism: the motion of molten rock under the surface of a planet, which results in volcanos.

wane: get smaller.

wax: get bigger.

Books

Andronik, Catherine M. *Great Minds of Science: Copernicus, Founder of Modern Astronomy.* Berkeley Heights, NJ: Enslow Publishers, 2002.

Berger, Melvin. *Discovering Jupiter: the Amazing Collision in Space.* New York: Scholastic, 1995.

Brown, Duncan, Ed. *The Visual Dictionary of the Universe.* New York: DK Publishing, 1993.

Campbell, Ann Jeanette. *Amazing Space.* New York: John Wiley and Sons, Inc., 1997.

Carson, Mary Kay. *Exploring the Solar System.* Chicago: Chicago Review Press, 2006.

Couper, Heather and Nigel Herbest. *How the Universe Works.* London: Dorling Kindersley Ltd., 1994.

Croswell, Ken. *Ten Worlds: Everything That Orbits the Sun.* Honesdale, PA: Boyds Mills Press, 2006.

Davis, Kenneth C. *Don't Know Much About Space.* New York: Harper Collins, 2001.

Dickinson, Terence. *Night Watch: A Practical Guide to Viewing the Universe.* Buffalo, NY: Firefly Books, 1998.

Ford, Harry. *The Young Astronomer.* New York: DK Publishing, 1998.

Fradin, Dennis Brindell. *Is There Life on Mars?* New York: Margaret K. McElderry Books, 1999.

Fradin, Dennis Brindell. *The Planet Hunters.* New York: Margaret K. McElderry Books, 1997.

Gallant, Roy A. *The Planets: Exploring the Solar System.* New York: Four Winds Press, 1982.

Hightower, Paul. *Galileo: Astronomer and Physicist.* Berkeley Heights, NJ: Enslow Publishers, 1997.

Kerrod, Robin and Sparrow, Giles. *The Way the Universe Works.* New York: DK Publishing, 2002.

Krull, Kathleen. *Giants of Science: Isaac Newton.* New York: Viking, 2006.

Lasky, Kathryn. *The Librarian Who Measured the Earth.* New York: Little, Brown and Co. 1994.

Lippencott, Kristen. *Eyewitness Science: Astronomy.* New York: DK Publishing, 1994.

Mechler, Gary. *First Field Guide to the Night Sky.* New York: Scholastic, 1999.

Miller, Robert and Wilson, Kenneth. *Making and Enjoying Telescopes.* New York: Sterling Press, 1995.

Pasachoff, Jay M. Peterson *First Guides: The Solar System.* Boston: Houghton Mifflin, 1990.

Rey, H.A. *The Stars: A New Way to See Them.* Boston: Houghton Mifflin, 1952.

Ride, Sally and O'Shaughnessy, Tam. *Exploring Our Solar System.* New York: Crown Publishers, 2003.

Roza, Greg. *The Incredible Story of Telescopes.* New York: Rosen Publishing Group, 2004.

Sobel, Dava. *The Planets.* New York: Penguin Books, 2005.

Schaff, Fred. *Planetology: Comparing Other Worlds to Our Own.* New York, Franklin Watts, 1996.

Scott, Elaine. *Close Encounters: Exploring the Universe with the Hubble Space Telescope.* New York: Hyperion Books for Children, 1998.

Steele, Philip. *Galileo: The Genius Who Faced the Inquisition.* Washington, DC: National Geographic Books, 2005.

Stott, Carole and Clint Twist. *1001 Facts about Space.* New York: Backpack Books, 2002.

Summers, Carolyn and Kerry Handron. *An Earthling's Guide to Deep Space.* New York: McGraw Hill, 1999.

Web Sites

Amateur Telescope Makers ➤ http://www.atmsite.org/

Astronomy magazine site ➤ http://www.astronomy.com

National Aeronautics and Space Administration ➤ http://www.nasa.gov/

NASA site on the search for other planets ➤ http://planetquest.jpl.nasa.gov/index.cfm

NASA site about rocketry ➤ http://exploration.grc.nasa.gov/education/rocket/shortr.html

NASA site that tracks spacecraft ➤ http://science.nasa.gov/Realtime/JTrack/Spacecraft.html

National Association of Rocketry ➤ http://www.nar.org/

The Planetary Society ➤ http://planetary.org/home/

The Search for Extraterrestrial Intelligence ➤ http://www.seti.housenet.org/

S.E.T.I at Home ➤ http://setiathome.berkeley.edu/

Space.com ➤ http://www.space.com

Sky and Telescope magazine ➤ http://skytonight.com/observing/highlights

Museums

Adler Planetarium and Astronomy Museum Chicago IL ➤ http://www.adlerplanetarium.org/

American Museum of Natural History, New York, NY ➤ http://www.amnh.org/

Buffalo Museum of Science Buffalo, Buffalo, NY ➤ http://www.sciencebuff.org/

California Science Center, Los Angeles, CA ➤ http://www.californiasciencecenter.org/

Center of Science and Industry, Columbus, OH ➤ http://www.cosi.org/

Cleveland Museum of Natural History Cleveland, OH
➤ http://www.cmnh.org/site/atthemuseum_planetariumandobservatory.aspx

Denver Museum of Nature and Science, Denver, CO. ➤ http://www.dmns.org/main/en/

Fernbank Science Center, Atlanta, GA ➤ http://fsc.fernbank.edu/

Franklin Institute Science Museum, Philadelphia, PA ➤ http://www2.fi.edu/

Kopernik Observatory and Science Education Center Vestal, NY ➤ http://http://www.kopernik.org/

Houston Museum of Natural Science, Houston, TX ➤ http://http://www.hmns.org/

Lawrence Hall of Science, Berkeley, CA ➤ http://http://www.lawrencehallofscience.org/

LodeStar Astronomy Center at the New Mexico Museum of Natural History and Science, Alburquerque, NM ➤ http://http://www.lodestar.unm.edu/shows.html

Miami Museum of Science and Planetarium Miami, FL ➤ http://http://www.miamisci.org/

Montshire Museum of Science Norwich, VT ➤ http://http://www.montshire.org/

Museum of Science, Boston, MA ➤ http://http://www.mos.org/

Museum of Science and Industry, Chicago, IL ➤ http://http://www.msichicago.org/

Pacific Science Center, Seattle, WA ➤ http://http://www.pacsci.org/

Reuben H. Fleet Science Center, San Diego, CA ➤ http://http://www.rhfleet.org/

Saint Louis Science Center, St. Louis, MO ➤ http://http://www.slsc.org/

Science Museum of Virginia, Richmond, VA ➤ http://http://www.smv.org/

Smithsonian National Air and Space Museum, Washington, DC ➤ http://http://www.nasm.si.edu/